Metal clay *magic*

Metal clay *magic*

Simple projects for making stunning silver jewellery at home

SARA DUTTON

First published in 2009 by New Holland Publishers (UK) Ltd
London · Cape Town · Sydney · Auckland

Garfield House, 86–88 Edgware Road, London W2 2EA, United Kingdom
www.newhollandpublishers.com

80 McKenzie Street, Cape Town 8001, South Africa
Unit 1, 66 Gibbes Street, Chatswood, NSW 2067, Australia
218 Lake Road, Northcote, Auckland, New Zealand

ISBN 978 1 84773 451 8

Senior Editor: **Louise Coe**
Production: **Laurence Poos**
Design: **Lisa Tai**
Photography: **Thomas Sultana**
Editorial Direction: **Rosemary Wilkinson**

10 9 8 7 6 5 4 3 2 1

Reproduction by PDQ Digital Media Solutions Ltd, UK
Printed and bound by Craft Print International Ltd, Singapore

Contents

Introduction

Metal clay is an incredibly versatile material made from fine silver (or gold) particles incorporated with a non-toxic organic binder. It is mouldable and can be shaped just like normal clay to take on many different shapes and textures. When it is fired, the binder burns away to leave the silver or gold, which will have taken on the shape and texture of the clay.

Due to its low firing temperature, metal clay can be incorporated with many different mediums and materials that can be fired along with it, such as ceramics, glass and cubic zirconia stones.

Metal clay has only been produced since the early 1990s, making it one of the newest crafts around. Although in its infancy (compared to the many traditional methods of making jewellery), it is becoming increasingly popular. There are a number of reasons for this: it is easy to work with and can produce relatively fast results, the tools required are inexpensive and easily sourced and the materials are easy to use and being improved all the time.

This book was written with the beginner in mind and it explains all of the basic techniques for working with metal clay in a straightforward and approachable way. It then provides a selection of fun projects for you try out the craft of metal clay for yourself. The projects vary in difficulty and have been marked 'beginner', 'intermediate' or 'advanced' accordingly, so you can start with something simple and then build your skills as you go along. They also make use of different techniques, ranging from making simple shapes with cutters to syringing and enamelling. You do not need any previous jewellery making experience to start working with metal clay – even children will enjoy working with it (although they should be supervised).

Once you are more familiar with the craft, you can try mixing and matching the different techniques and embellishing them as you wish to create your own unique designs and pieces. Remember to relax, enjoy this fantastic material and have a lot of fun along the way.

The basics

Materials, tools and equipment

On the following pages you will find information on the various clay types, highlighting their different properties and uses. Many of the tools needed are items you may already have at home, some you will need to source from hardware or craft shops.

Basic techniques

This section explains the basic techniques that are used throughout the projects, with clear instructions and step-by-step photographs. Use these pages as an easy reference guide when working through the book.

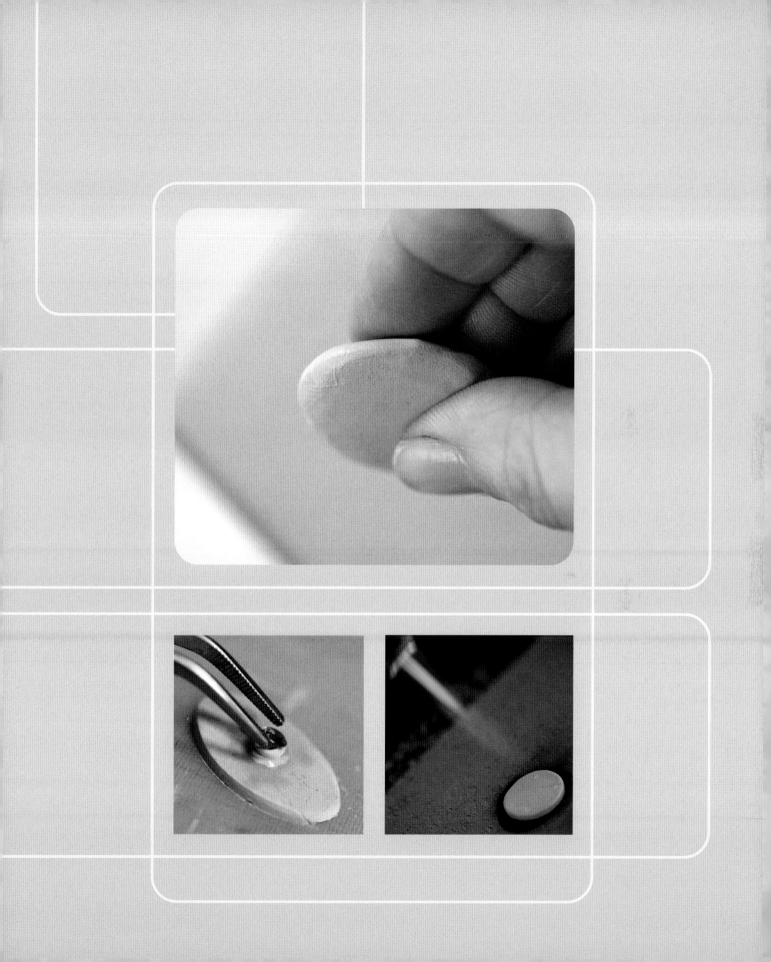

Materials

Clay

There are two manufacturers of metal clay: Aida Chemicals Industries Co Ltd, which produces 'Art Clay', and Mitsubishi Materials Corporation, which manufactures 'PMC' (precious metal clay). Both of these clays can be used to produce the same results, however the firing times and properties of the clays are slightly different so you should make sure that you use the firing schedules set by the manufacturer. Throughout this book I have used PMC, but Art Clay can also be used.

The main type of metal clay used is silver clay. This is available in four different formats: lump clay, paste, syringe and sheet clay. Each of these gives a variety of properties and can be used to different effect.

SILVER LUMP CLAY

This is a solid block of clay and is the building block for many items. It comes in a few different formats, which varying properties:

- **PMC3**: This is the newest generation of silver clay. It shrinks by approximately 12%, has the slowest drying time – allowing you to work with the product for longer while still pliable – and fires very quickly at a low temperature, making it ideal for using with glass.
- **PMC+**: This clay shrinks by 12%. It is drier and of a heavier texture than PMC3. It is great for fingerprinting as it captures textures very well.
- **PMC Standard Clay**: The first PMC clay on the market, this clay shrinks by 30% so it is good for making a big piece with a lot of detail, but

is not good for rings. This clay needs to be fired for 2 hours so cannot be fired with a blowtorch.

- **Art Clay 650**: This silver clay shrinks by 8–10%.
- **Art Clay 650 Slow Dry**: This clay shrinks by 8–10% but gives you slightly longer working time than Art Clay 650.
- **Art Clay Silver Original**: The first Art Clay on the market, this is similar to art clay 650, but requires firing at a much higher temperature.
- **Art Clay Silver Slow Dry**: this clay is much like Art Clay Silver Original, but it has a longer working time.

SILVER PASTE

Paste is a liquid version of silver clay and is slightly more liquid than the syringe clay (see below). It is used for binding clay sections together, mending and filling gaps, attaching bails and using with leaves and core materials, such as covering cork clay.

Paste can be made by mixing together lump clay and water. It is also available in PMC3, PMC+ and Art Clay 650. Pastes should only be used with the same type of lump clay unless the silver has been fired.

SILVER CLAY SYRINGE

Silver clay can also be bought in a syringe, ready for piping out lines or patterns. This clay has a thicker consistency than the paste version. It is excellent for decorating lump clay, setting stones and creating beads and rings. It is available in PMC3, PMC+ and Art Clay 650.

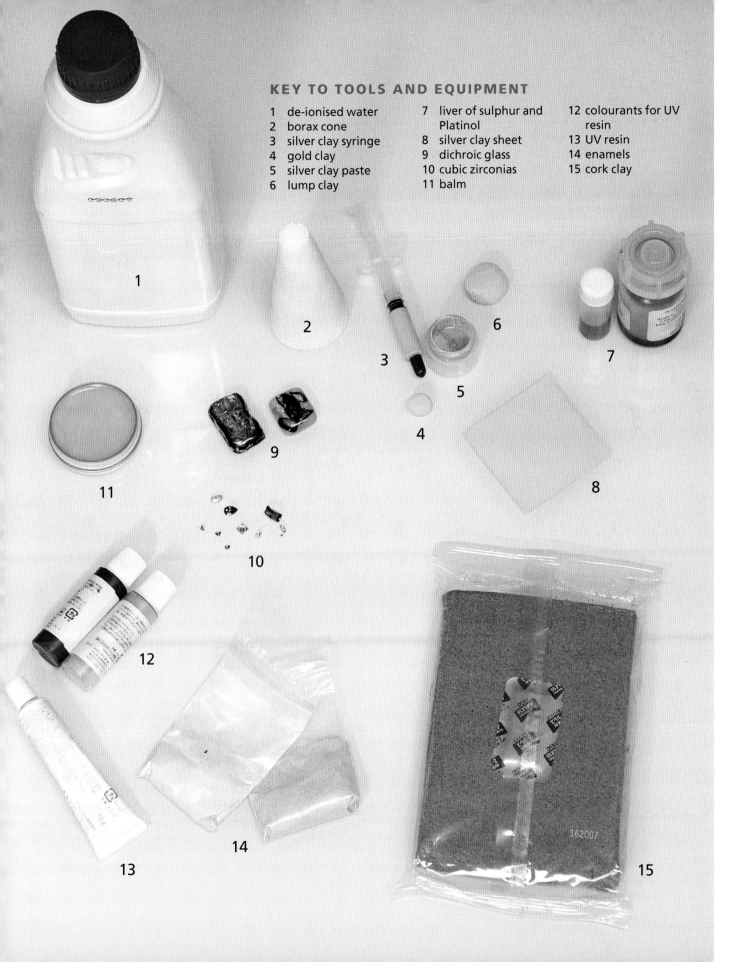

KEY TO TOOLS AND EQUIPMENT

1 de-ionised water
2 borax cone
3 silver clay syringe
4 gold clay
5 silver clay paste
6 lump clay
7 liver of sulphur and Platinol
8 silver clay sheet
9 dichroic glass
10 cubic zirconias
11 balm
12 colourants for UV resin
13 UV resin
14 enamels
15 cork clay

SILVER SHEET CLAY

A thin, flexible sheet of clay can be used be produce pleats and folds, reminiscent of fabric. It can be used to produce origami shapes as it can be cut with scissors and craft cutters. It should not be used with water until fired or it will degrade. It is available in PMC+ Sheet and Art Clay + Paper.

SILVER CLAY OIL PASTE

This is an oil-based clay paste can be used to attach fired pieces together. It must be kiln fired. It is only available in Art Clay.

GOLD CLAY

Gold clay can also be used to make jewellery, but it is very expensive so is best used to decorate silver or to make very small pieces. The projects in this book focus on silver clay, but you can embellish your pieces with gold clay. There are two gold lump clays available on the market: PMC Gold Clay 22k shrinks by 14% and can be fired at both high and low temperatures. The higher firing temperature is unsuitable for combining with silver clay. Art Clay Gold Clay 22k, shrinks by 15% and requires a high firing temperature. Neither are suitable for torch firing.

You can also buy gold paste. This has various application methods, so you should carefully check the manufacturer's instructions on the packet. It is available in Art Clay and Aura 22 PMC.

CORK CLAY

This can be used for making hollow shapes. The metal clay is wrapped around the cork clay and when it is fired the cork burns away. This must be fired in a kiln.

drawing patterns onto sheet clay using pencil

this hollow heart shape was created using cork clay

Balm

Balm is a very important part of the metal clay process as it helps to keep the clay moist. It should be applied to hands before working with the clay. It should also be applied very lightly to the work board if it is not a non-stick surface. Do not use too much balm; just enough to stop it sticking is all that is required.
The balm must have a vegetable base, such as olive oil or badger balm. Be careful to avoid petroleum-based balms, as they will interfere with the clay.

Other materials

Various other materials can be incorporated into your metal clay work to add texture, colour and decoration. Some of these can be fired with the clay and others need to be applied after firing.

ADDING SURFACE COLOUR

There are many ways to add colour to your silver pieces. Chemical agents, such as liver of sulphur and Platinol can add iridescent colours. UV Resins or two-part epoxy resins can be added with acrylic for vibrant colours. Enamels can add bright colours with a shiny finish. Gold Leaf can also be applied to silver clay once it has been fired – this technique is known as Keum-Boo.

SETTING STONES AND GLASS

Most natural stones cannot be fired so need to be set into the clay after firing. This can be done using bezel wire. Man-made stones such as cubic zirconias can usually be fired with a torch and kiln, but should not be quenched in water. Cubic zirconias come in a splendid range of colours, but not all colours are colour-safe when fired. Always check with the supplier before firing. Swarovski crystals cannot be fired in the kiln and should be attached afterwards.

use your finger to apply balm to rolled out clay

Pieces of dichroic glass make great decorations and are great for firing with low-fire temperature metal clay on a slow fire in kiln.

JEWELLERY FINDINGS

Findings such as silver eyelets, earring posts and brooch backs can be added to the clay before firing. Jump rings, clasps and brooch pins should be added after firing to finish off the piece. It is always useful to have fine silver wire and silver eyelets are very handy for attaching a pendant to a jump ring, for example.

Tools and equipment

The list of tools for metal clay could be endless as you can use so many things, from tools associated with more traditional metal working and tools for modelling clay to household items and nail files from the local store. Please don't feel that you need everything listed here; you can improvise and build your tool kit to suit your own needs.

Sculpting and shaping wet clay

It is best to work on a **work board** rather than a table – it is easier to clean and means that you can move your clay around, for example if you want to dry a piece somewhere else. Suitable items for work boards are: a **plastic page holder**, a **laminate surface**, **Teflon** (non-stick baking surface), a **ceramic tile** or a **craft mat**.

To roll out the clay you will need a **roller**, such as an **acrylic roller**, **snake roller** or **perspex square**. You will also need to use **spacers**, such as **acrylic spacer bars** or layers of **playing cards** to determine the thickness of the clay you are rolling out. These should be placed either side of the clay while you are rolling.

You can create shapes in the clay with the use of **craft cutters** and **cookie cutters** or by creating your own moulds from a **moulding compound**, such as a **two-part moulding compound**. You can also create textures in the clay using **rubber stamps**, **rubber** or **brass texture mats** or even with textured items, such as **lace**, **leaves** and **household items**.

Paintbrushes and **clay shapers** are useful for shaping the clay and shapes can be carved into the clay using a **needle tool**, a **metal scriber** (for making

KEY TO TOOLS AND EQUIPMENT

1	wire cutters
2/3/4	jewellery pliers
5	borax dish
6	pestle and mortar
7	straw
8	pencil
9/10	carving tools
11	clay shaper
12	hand drill
13	rubber block
14	florists block and pipe cleaners
15	fine silver wire
16	brass brush
17	stainless steel brush
18	bail brush
19	agate burnisher
20	metal burnisher
21	metal scriber
22	paintbrush
23/24	metal files
25	needle tool
26	earring wires
27	eyelets
28	jump rings
29	cotton buds
30	ring mandrel and sizer
31	tape measure
32	cord
33	acrylic spacer bars
34	acrylic roller
35	mould
36	craft cutter
37/38	cookie cutters
39	silicon two part moulder
40	reverse action tweezers
41	tweezers
42	scissors
43	ruler
44	silver polishing cloth
45	graded polishing papers
46	Teflon
47	brass texture mat
48	rubber texture mat
49	playing cards

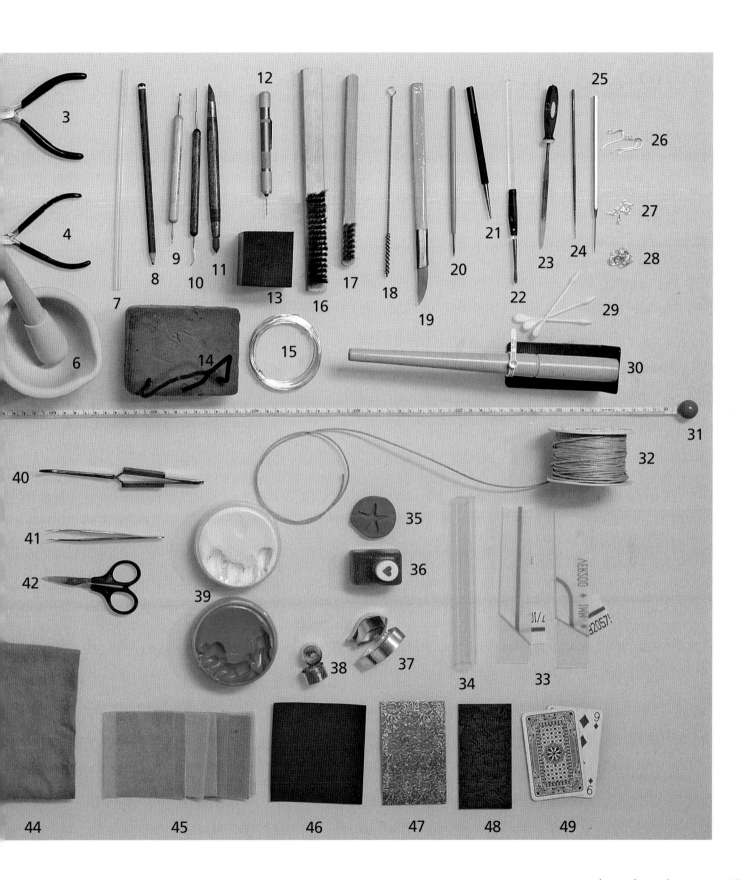

marks on metal) and **carving tools**.

Sheet clay can be cut using **scissors** and glued using **white craft glue**.

If you are creating rings, you will need to use a **ring sizer** and **mandrel** to achieve the right size. If you are creating bails for your jewellery you will need small pieces of **straws** to help shape the clay.

Tools for manipulating dry clay

Once the clay has dried you can file the hardened shapes with **metal files**, **nail files**, **buffer nail boards**, **sanding pads** and **sandpaper**.

Firing

There are two methods of firing your clay pieces: in a **kiln** or by hand with a **blowtorch**.

If using a **kiln,** you will find that they come in a variety of sizes – do think about what you might be using it for and where in your home you will be setting it up before buying. You will need to wear **protective kiln gloves** and use **kiln tongs** to remove the fired pieces. Place delicate objects on a **kiln pillow** before placing them in the kiln.

A **small butane gas torch** is suitable for firing by hand. You will need a torch that can get to 1300°C (2372°F) and that has an adjustable flame. A safety lock is also useful.

You should wear **safety glasses** and **protective gloves** and should fire the clay on a **fire brick** or **soldering block** on top of a **heatproof surface**, such as a **ceramic tile**. Use **solder tweezers** to move hot pieces.

Finishing fired clay

After firing, **stainless steel** and **brass** wire **brushes** are used to remove the white fire scale.

The clay can be given a higher polish with the use of **metal** or **agate burnishers**, **polishing pads** (which come in various grades), **polishing papers** and **cloths** and **silver polish**. You can also use a **tumbler** and **stainless steel mixed shot**. The drum of the tumbler rotates causing the silver to tumble over – during this process the structure of the fine silver hardens slightly, helping to produce an even shine.

General craft tools

If you are attaching findings to your jewellery, such as jump rings, you will need to use **jewellery pliers**. To make holes in the pieces to attach jump rings and findings you will need to use a **drill**. It is advisable to drill onto a suitable surface, such as a **rubber block**. You will also need **wire cutters** for working with wire. An assorted range of different types and sizes of **tweezers** are also useful.

KEY TO TOOLS AND EQUIPMENT

1. kiln
2. UV lamp
3. hot plate
4. kiln pillow and shelf and torch block
5. fire extinguisher
6. tumbler with barrel
7. rotary tool for sanding and polishing
8. safety goggles
9. wire mesh
10. kiln tongs
11. third hand
12. blow torch

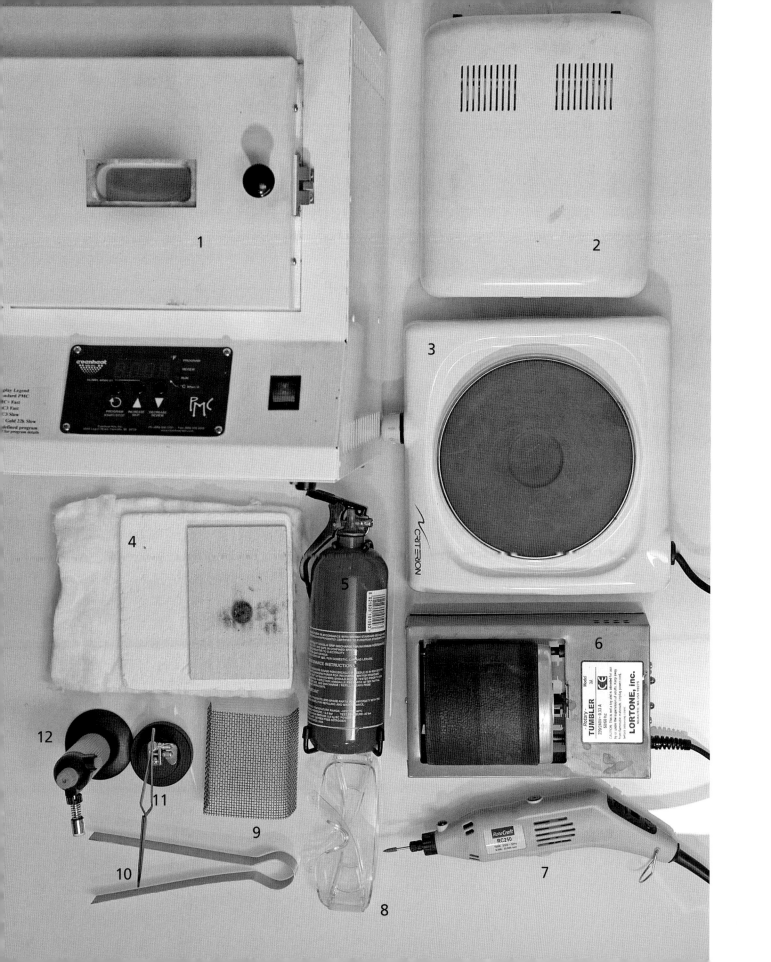

1

2

3

4

5

6

7

8

9

10

11

12

Basic techniques

Before you embark upon the projects in this book, it is important that you familiarize yourself with the basic techniques of working with metal clay. It is a good idea to experiment with both manipulating and firing the clay so you feel fully comfortable working with it and are ready to try out some of the intermediate and advanced projects in the book.

Working with wet clay

As the clay dries out quickly, it is best to use the same size packet of lump clay as the amount required for the jewellery project. Any excess clay should be wrapped up in cling film as soon as possible and returned to the resealable packet or an airtight container. Placing a small piece of wet sponge or cloth into the packet or container will help to keep it moist. Even then, however, the clay will dry out so do not save it for a rainy day.

If the clay becomes rock hard you can make it into paste by grinding it down into a powder, then placing it in a small container and stirring water into it until you achieve the right consistency.

If cracks start to appear in the clay and it is becoming stiff, roll the clay out into a thin layer and add a fine layer of water over the surface of the clay, then fold the clay in half. Add another fine layer of water and fold again. Place the clay into some cling film and knead with your fingers. If the texture is still too sticky, give the clay a couple of quick turns in your hands and flatten slightly.

In hot weather a fine mist of water from a spray bottle can help extend the moisture content.

Health and Safety

- Work in a well-ventilated room.
- Wash your hands after using the clay, especially before eating.
- Don't eat at your workstation.
- The kiln is hot so do not touch the sides and back.
- Don't place anything on top of your kiln.
- Tie long hair back and do not wear baggy sleeves when torch firing.
- Wear toe-covered shoes in the workshop.
- Use solder tweezers to move hot pieces of silver about.
- Wear safety goggles when firing.
- Keep a small fire extinguisher handy.
- Follow the manufacturer's instructions when using chemicals.
- Wear a dust/fume mask when using dry enamels, two-part epoxy resins and when removing Ceramic fibre paper.
- A glass brush should be used under running water and gloves should be worn as the fibres are an irritant.
- Wear UV glasses if firing enamels for a long period.
- Dispose of chemicals and enamels safely.
- Work in a tidy environment; accidents and spills are less likely to happen.

ROLLING THE CLAY

This simple technique is very easy to master. It is important to ensure that the clay is evenly rolled out to give you a good base for making your item.

To determine the thickness of the clay it is best to use acrylic spacer bars or layers of playing cards either side of the clay while rolling. One spacer bar or four playing cards placed either side of the clay will give you a piece with the depth of 1 mm.

Tip

❀ **Move cut clay shapes with a damp paintbrush so you do not get finger marks in the clay.**

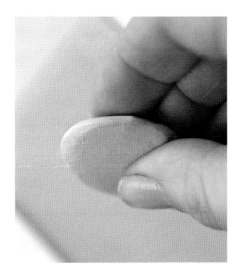

1 Apply a small amount of balm to your hands and the work board. If using PMC, roll the clay firmly between the palms of your hands to warm it slightly and soften it. If using Art Clay, just knead it with your fingers a couple of times as the clay can be slightly drier. Take care not to over roll or you will dry the clay out. Then, place the clay on the work board and put spacer bars or cards on either side of the clay.

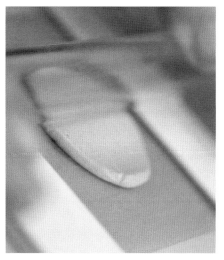

2 Roll out firmly using a roller, then move the spacer bars or cards and rotate your work board. Replace the spacer bars or cards and roll again. This ensures that the clay is rolled out evenly.

SYRINGING

To extrude the clay from a syringe, hold the bottom of the syringe with one hand and hold the top with the other, then press down with your thumb to push out the clay. Holding the syringe tip approximately 3– 4 cm (1¼–1½ in) away from the clay base will give enough height to allow the syringed clay to drop slowly and give you more control of where it is being placed.

most syringes come with a syringe cap or tip

APPLYING TEXTURE

It is easy to add a texture to your rolled-out clay. All you need to do is apply a thin layer of balm over the clay surface, then place the textured item on top and press gently. Alternatively, you can use a texture mat. After applying a thin layer of balm, place the mat over the clay and then gently roll over the mat with a roller or with even pressure from your fingertips. Remove carefully.

MAKING LOOPED BAILS

Looped bails can be attached to your pendant to allow a chain or ribbon to be strung through. When you attach your bail, make sure that the clay pendant is dry or it will distort its shape and could break from the pressure of applying the bail.

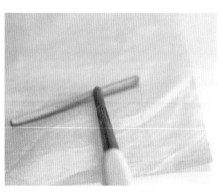

1 Cut a very small piece of clay and place it on the work board. Wrap the rest up and return to a sealable packet. Roll into a ball by placing a snake roller or a small acrylic or perspex square on top and making small circular motions, with fingers on the side of the square. Next, roll the clay quickly from side to side with the roller to create a long, thin sausage shape.

2 Apply a thin layer of water over the surface of the sausage with a paintbrush and let the water absorb.

Tip

❀ Do not try to use the clay sausage until the water has absorbed or it will be so slippery you that you will have no control over it. To blend bails, dampen your clay shaper with water first, it is much easier to blend with than when it is dry.

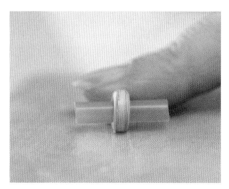

3 Place a small piece of a straw in the centre of the sausage and apply a thick coat of paste to either end.

4 Bring one end of the sausage over the straw to sit on top of the other end and press down with a finger for a couple of minutes.

5 Trim the sausage, then apply paste to the bail loop and to the part of the item you will be attaching the bail to. Press the two pieces together for a couple of minutes.

6 Cut off any excess clay from the back and then use a damp clay shaper to blend by smoothing the bail into the other surface. Take care not to remove too much as it is holding on the bail.

7 Allow to dry, then remove the straw with a gentle twisting motion. Fill any gaps with paste and dry again. When dry, sand and fire.

MAKING BRIDGE BAILS

Bridge bails sit behind a piece rather than on top, so they do not interfere with the main shape of the jewellery.

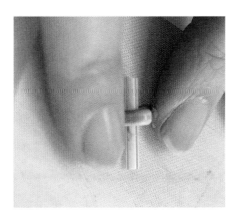

1 As with the looped bail, form a long sausage shape, apply water and let it sink in. Place a small section of a straw onto your work board and lay the clay over the straw, then press down on either side to form a bridge.

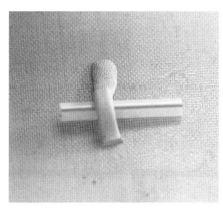

2 Cut off the excess clay and allow to dry. When dry, remove the straw and attach to the main piece using a good thick blob of paste.

Tip

❀ Make sure your bails are completely dry before you remove the straw or you will risk breaking them.

Setting cubic zirconias

These gemstones must be set so that they sit just below the surface of the clay to ensure that the stone is not pushed out when the clay shrinks. Small cubic zirconias can be simply pushed gently into the clay with a tip, such as a needle tool. Larger stones that are to be set into a shallow piece of clay cannot simply be pushed in or they might distort the surface of the clay. They should be set using the 'doughnut setting method', as follows:

1 Remove a plug of clay that is smaller than the stone circumference. This can be done by inserting a small straw into the clay and twisting slightly to pull out a plug of clay.

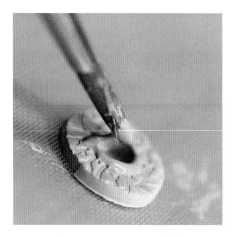

2 Apply some paste around the edge of the hole using a paintbrush.

3 Syringe a ring around the edge of the hole. Press down gently with the edge of a damp paintbrush to make sure the syringed ring is attached to the base.

4 Press the cubic zirconia into the hole so that it sits slightly lower than the clay surface.

Tip

❀ If you get some clay on your stone, leave it until the clay dries before trying to remove it, or you will spread the clay over the stone, making it harder to remove. Use a clay shaper and a cotton bud for cleaning the stone up.

Working with dry clay

It is important to dry clay thoroughly before firing or the shape can distort and crack. The length of time taken for the clay to dry naturally depends on various factors, such as how warm the room you are working in is, which clay has been used and how thick the clay piece is. The drying time is normally about 24 hours. There are ways to help speed up this process, such as placing the clay on a hotplate, in a food rehydrator or even in a warm airing cupboard, to name just a few.

To check that the piece is completely dry, place it on a mirror and leave for a few minutes. If there are moisture traces left, it is still damp. Do not put warm pieces on a mirror or you will produce condensation.

Once your clay is dry you can join pieces together, file and sand shapes and drill holes in them, ready for firing. Dry clay can still be broken at this stage, so do not press too hard when filing or drilling.

JOINING PIECES

To join two pieces of clay together, apply paste to the areas of both sides that will be in contact with each other. Any paste that squeezes out can be removed with a damp paintbrush. If you have excess lump clay you can blend it in using a dampened clay shaper. The joined pieces should then be left to dry thoroughly before firing.

FILING AND SANDING

You can clear up the edges of the piece and smooth down the surfaces before firing by using various files and sandpapers. Start with the coarser grain file and end up with a fine grain paper. You must ensure that the clay is completely dry before firing or sanding or you risk breaking it. Do not press too hard as the dry clay is still breakable.

ENGRAVING

To engrave your piece, draw a design in pencil on the dry clay, then follow the design with a carver or inscriber to carve out the pattern. Carefully remove any shavings with a dry paintbrush.

DRILLING

To make a hole in the clay, you will need to place the clay onto a rubber block and use a hand drill. Turn the drill in one direction and let the weight of the drill take it through the clay. When it is nearly through, the clay piece will start to turn, so place a hand onto it to secure it. After a few more full turns the drill should be through the clay. To release the drill, just pump up and down slowly and pull it out.

Tip

❀ You can also drill metal clay after it has been fired with a hand drill; you just have to apply some pressure.

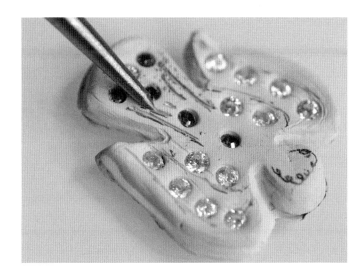

carving a design onto dry clay

Attachments

To attach findings, such as fine silver eyelets, bails, earring posts and brooch backs, use a thick blob of paste to attach and allow to dry. Then re-apply more paste to make the bond nice and strong. Allow to dry, then fire. Fine silver wire can also be fired into place without having to worry about dark oxidisation taking place, which happens with sterling silver. You can also create your own wire attachments by bending fine silver wire into your desired shape.

Tip

✿ If you are using a clay that allows you to fire on a low-temperature, slow-fire programme on your kiln below 650°C (1200°F), then sterling silver findings can be used. These must be cooled naturally. Use a stainless steel brush and a tumbler to remove any mild oxidation formed when firing.

use a paintbrush to apply paste when attaching eyelets

Firing

Using a kiln or torch firing are suitable for different projects. Kiln firing offers more options for incorporating materials with the clay, such as glass and cork clay. Torch firing is possible on many different shapes up to a 40 cm (16 in) diameter. Oval and round shapes and clay pieces with an even depth are easier to hold at a constant temperature which is important when torch firing.

Always move hot silver pieces with tongs or solder tweezers and make sure there is a suitable place to put the hot article down. You can quench silver in water to cool it quickly, but never do this if the piece has stones in, or you will fracture the stones.

For safety, please ensure that you are wearing safety goggles when firing and loose hair or clothes are kept out of the way.

USING A KILN

When choosing a kiln, make sure that it is compatible with the materials you want to work with. Always follow the manufacturer's instructions and make sure that you wear protective kiln gloves and safety goggles and use kiln tongs.

TORCH FIRING

Torch firing is suitable for small items of an even thickness, such as pendants and rings. Items that are unsuitable for torch firing include sheet clay, glass, natural stones and combustible core materials, such as cork clay.

When the clay is completely dry, place on a fire brick or soldering block, and stand this on a heatproof surface, such as a ceramic tile. Ignite your blowtorch so that the blue inner flame is 4 cm (1½ in) long and the yellow flame 2.5 cm (1 in) longer. Move the blowtorch in a circular motion over the top of the clay. First you

using a blowtorch to fire silver clay

will see some smoke and then a flame – this is the non toxic binder burning away. When it has reached the sintering stage it will be glowing a pale orange (the colour of smoked salmon). Keep this colour evenly for at least 2 minutes.

You can either leave your piece to cool naturally or you can quench in water. Never quench pieces that have stones set in them as they will fracture.

Tips

✿ Use solder tweezers to move hot pieces.

✿ When the clay reaches a pale orange colour ('sintering') then you can set a timer for at least 2 minutes. Different makes of clay vary very slightly, so check the manufacturer's firing schedule. You can over-fire clay but you must not under-fire.

✿ If you see a flash of silver, the piece is getting too hot, so you need to widen the circular motion slightly until the temperature drops a little.

Finishing your clay items
BRUSHING

Once the fired item has cooled, use a stainless steel brush to remove the white fire scale from the piece by brushing in small circular motions. This will give you a lovely satin finish and will also help to harden the silver.

BURNISHING

Once all of the fire scale has been removed you can use a stainless steel or agate burnisher to highlight areas into a high shine by using the side of the burnisher with a small hard circular motion.

Never use the tip of the burnisher; it will scratch the surface badly.

POLISHING PAPERS

You can use polishing papers or cloths to smoothen and polish the surface of the item, giving a fantastic, if somewhat labour-intensive, finish.

The papers come in different grades and you should start with the lowest grade first, polishing in small strokes in one direction. Then use the next finer grade paper and work across the lines in the opposite direction until you cannot see the lines from the previous paper. Continue until you reach the last paper grade, then work in small circular motions until all of the lines are removed. Finally, give a polish with some silver polish for a great shiny finish.

Tip

✿ Wrap polishing paper around a buffing nail file for extra pressure.

✿ If you have created a high shine and decide you want a satin finish, just use your stainless steel or brass brush again.

LIVER OF SULPHUR

This is a surface dye that can create iridescent colours on silver. To use, wash the silver piece in a little baking soda or liquid detergent to remove any dirt. Put a few drops of liquid liver of sulphur (or, if using a dry version, a pea-size amount) into hot but not boiling water. Then dip the silver into the liver of sulphur using tweezers, or apply in small areas where needed with a paintbrush. Rinse in cold water (running water is best) to fix the colour.

Tips

❀ The colours produced using liver of sulphur are golden to ambers, reds to purples then greens to black. Rinsing in cold water will help fix the colour but it will change over time, as it is not stable colour.

❀ Liver of sulphur can be removed, however a pewter shade is usually left behind since the silver is still porous.

use tweezers to dip your piece into the liver of sulphur

of the silver, which could cause the enamel to crack and 'ping' off. If you are using a piece of fine silver that is thicker than 1.3 mm you will not need to apply a counter-enamel. This works best with round or oval shapes. Rectangular shapes often benefit from using a counter enamel as the corners make them more fragile.

ENAMELLING

Enamels are coloured glass, composed of silicates. They can produce bright, vivid colours with a glossy finish to decorate your silver pieces. These can only be fired in a kiln. You can buy enamels in an unground or powdered form. For ease of use, powdered enamels are preferable, but I would still re-grind these with a pestle and mortar and a small amount of water to give a smoother and more even finish.

Enamel often requires the application of a counter-enamel on the back of the piece. This is just a layer of enamel applied to the back of the piece. It means the expansion of the piece is even and prevents distortion

Preparing the enamel

To prepare enamel, put a small amount of enamel powder into a mortar and add a little tap water to cover. Place a cloth over the bowl and grind the powder until it is smooth (the sound will be less gritty as it breaks down) and of an even size, then tip the water away. Wash the powder by covering with distilled water, tap the side of the bowl and wait a few moments for the particles to settle, then pour the cloudy water off. Repeat this washing process until the water becomes clear. Store in small containers with lids, it is best to use on the day of washing so only grind small amounts at a time.

Preparing your silver for enamelling

Before enamelling a piece of fired silver, you should wash it thoroughly under running water with either a wire brush or a glass brush with pumice powder. Glass brushes shed fibres, so unless you do this under running water it can cause painful irritation. You should then take your piece with tweezers to the kiln and just warm off the piece. Avoid touching the silver piece with your hands or you may impart oils onto it that can discolour the enamel.

Applying enamel

When you transfer the washed enamel to the container it will still have a small amount of water around it. This is helpful as it will help the wet enamel powder to be applied evenly. It also stops glass particles floating around in the air.

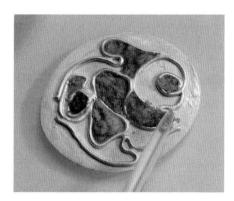 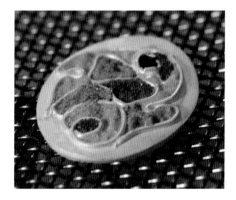 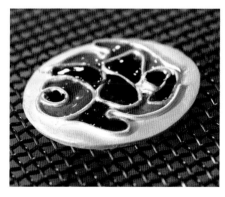

1 Lay down the wet enamel by using either a brush or a straw that has been cut into a point. Pick up the enamel with the straw or brush from the container and transfer to the silver piece. Tap the side of the piece gently to even out the enamel. Allow to dry.

2 Fire in a kiln at about 850°C (1560°F) for approximately 30 to 90 seconds, until the enamel looks like crystallized sugar grains.

3 Repeat ideally two more times; on the last firing the enamel should look smooth and glossy.

RESIN

Resin is a polymer plastic and can be used to capture inclusions, such as acrylic paint, when making jewellery. It can be drilled and sanded when hard. Resin comes in two different formats. There is UV resin and a two-part epoxy resin. There are advantages and disadvantages to both systems.

Firstly, UV resin is low-odour resin. You can cover the surface of a piece in many different layers of colours within an afternoon. A UV light box is needed to cure each layer of colour; this takes 3 to 5 minutes under a UV light. The disadvantages are that it is not so good at building blocks of resin for jewellery.

Two-part epoxy resin has a stronger odour, which can be an irritant when breathing in. It is best to wear a fume mask when using. This resin produces heat when mixed, so should only be mixed in a small amount at a time and should be disposed of in a separate metal bin (not your household one). It takes longer to cure. The advantages are that you can make bracelets and blocks of resin jewellery as it sets harder

in a bigger form than UV resin. You also don't need a light box. Two-part epoxys vary slightly from manufacturer to manufacturer, so check the instructions for mixing.

The instructions in this book are for UV resins. If using two-part epoxy resins, please refer to the manufacturer's instructions as these can vary slightly on mixing and curing times.

Tips

❀ It is better to build thin layers of resin and cure in between each one, building up the depth of tones and colours. This is because if there is a lot of colour pigment it can effect the curing. I usually put just a very thin layer of clear UV resin for the top layer and cure for my final layer under a UV lamp.

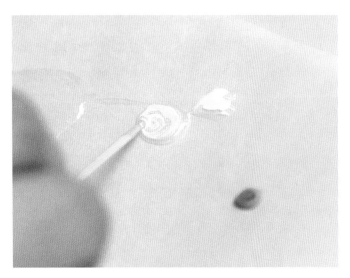

1 Place a small amount of the clear UV resin jelly on a tile or baking parchment and, using a cocktail stick, blend a small amount of acrylic colour into this.

2 Apply this to your finished piece of jewellery and cure under a UV light.

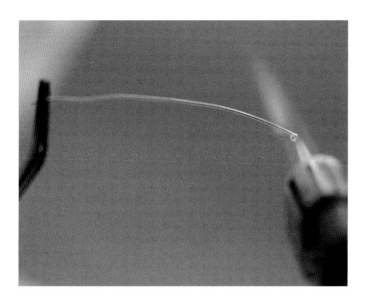

balling ends of silver wire will make lovely head pins

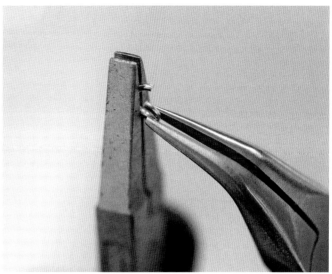

how to close a jump ring

SOLDERING

Soldering is a means to attach sterling silver findings to your fine silver. Sterling silver findings are harder wearing than fine silver. You need silver solder wire, which acts as a bond to bind the two surfaces together, and a flux, which is a chemical that helps the flow of the solder towards the heat of the torch. A silver solder strip is used as a filler to bond two silver pieces together. Silver soldering cannot be accomplished without the use of a flux. Make sure that you wear goggles at all times when soldering and do not pick up hot items without tongs.

BALLING FINE SILVER WIRE

You can create attractive balls on the ends of the silver wire to be used for making head pins or decorative finishes. To do this, hold the wire with tweezers at an angle onto the tip of the blue flame of a blowtorch. After a short while the tip of the wire will form a ball.

ATTACHING A JUMP RING

To fix findings onto your jewellery you will need to attach jump rings to the bails or holes in the pieces. To open a jump ring, hold one side of the jump ring with a pair of flat nose pliers, then open the jump ring up with a pair of jewellery pliers by pulling the other side towards you. To close, push the side you opened up towards you, then back slightly past the other wire and then forward, pushing in slightly as you do until the wire lightly rubs together with other side.

The projects

Now you are ready to tackle some beautiful projects. Start with a beginner project and then work your way through the intermediate and finally the advanced projects. All of them are clearly explained with tools and materials listed to help you get started. They cover a variety of techniques that will enable you to explore metal clay and give you the knowledge and inspiration eventually to create your own designs.

Textured leaf pendant

This simple beginner's project uses real leaves and a leaf cutter to add texture and shape to the clay. String the pendant onto a length of ribbon or cord of your choice; here both a thin green ribbon and a green cord have been used for a double-layered effect.

Skill level: **Beginner** ★

MATERIALS
- balm
- 25 g (1 oz) silver clay
- 2 small leaves with good veining on the underside
- silver clay paste
- 40 to 46 cm (16 to 18 in) ribbon or cord, depending on desired length of finished necklace
- 2 silver cord endings
- 2 jump rings (5 mm)
- 1 clasp

TOOLS
- work board
- spacer bars or 8 playing cards
- acrylic roller
- tweezers
- leaf cutters
- paintbrush
- perspex square or snake roller
- straw
- clay shaper for attaching the bail
- files
- sandpaper
- kiln
- stainless steel brush
- metal or agate burnisher (optional)
- jewellery pliers

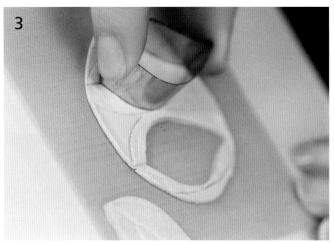

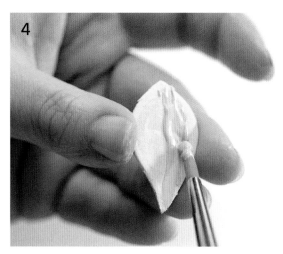

Tips

✿ If the clay gets stuck in the cutter, use the side of a damp paintbrush to push out the shape.

✿ It is a good idea to use a leaf with a shiny texture so that it is not necessary to apply balm to the clay surface.

✿ If you do not have a leaf cutter, you can cut out leaf shapes using a craft knife instead.

to make the pendant

1 Apply a small amount of balm to your hands, open the clay packet and pinch out a small piece of clay for bail and a piece for the pendant. Wrap the clay for the bail up in plastic and seal in packet. Place the clay for the pendant on the work board and place spacer bars or 4 playing cards on either side of the clay. Using the roller, firmly roll out the clay.

2 Place the underside of the leaves side by side down onto the surface of the clay and roll over them to create an impression in the clay. Remove the leaves with tweezers.

3 Cut the leaf shapes out using cutters. Allow the clay to dry thoroughly.

4 Apply a very thick layer of paste to the underside of the leaf that will be sat on top using a paintbrush.

5 Join the two pieces together carefully. Remove the excess paste with a damp paintbrush and allow the piece to dry.

6 Make the bail and attach to main leaf shape, following the basic looped bail instructions on page 20.

7 Allow to dry, then remove the straw and fill any gaps with paste. Allow to dry again, then file and sand any rough edges with a sanding file or sandpaper.

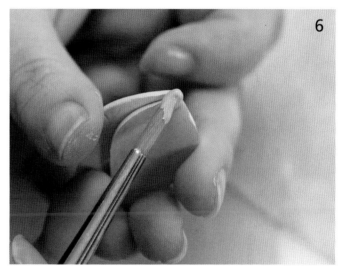

8 Fire in a kiln according to the manufacturer's instructions. When the piece has cooled after firing, remove the white fire scale with a stainless steel brush. Brush using firm circular movements.

9 If a high-shine finish is desired, burnish with a metal or agate burnisher to avoid scratches. Use the side of the burnisher and small, firm circular movements.

10 Thread the ribbon or cord through the bail and secure with silver cord endings. Add a jump ring to each end using jewellery pliers (see page 29), attaching a clasp to one end.

Tips

✿ If you decide to use a small leaf cutter, it is possible to use a blow torch for firing.

✿ Dip the leaves into liver of sulphur to give them some colour.

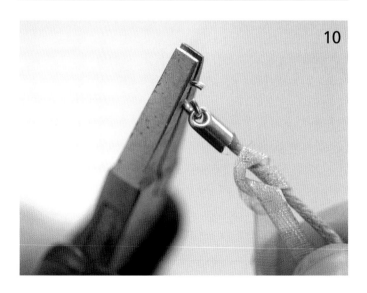

Variation

For earrings, use a smaller-sized cutter and a smaller amount of clay. Attach eyelets and earring wires to finish.

Split coil ring

This attractive, made-to-measure ring encases four cubic zirconias. It is a very good beginner's ring shape and can be easily adapted for different looks. You may even choose to leave it as an interesting silver band with no stones added at all.

Skill level: **Beginner** ★

MATERIALS
- balm
- 9 g (¼ oz) silver clay, cut in half
- silver clay paste
- 4 x 3 mm (⅛ in) cubic zirconias

TOOLS
- ring sizer
- strip of paper
- ring mandrel
- adhesive tape
- pencil
- work board
- perspex square
- needle tool or cutter
- paintbrush
- tweezers
- files
- sandpaper
- kiln or blowtorch
- stainless steel brush
- metal or agate burnisher

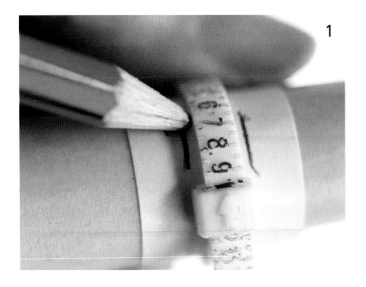

to make the coil ring

1 Measure the finger with a ring sizer and add two sizes; this will allow for shrinkage. Place a strip of paper around the ring mandrel and use a small piece of adhesive tape to hold in place. This needs to be a snug fit, but not so tight that it can't be slid it off later. Slide the ring sizer onto the paper on the mandrel and mark with pencil where it sits.

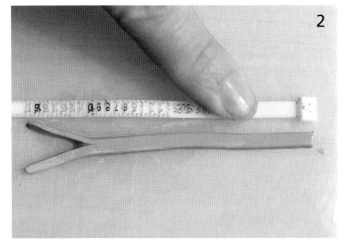

2 Apply balm to hands, then roll the clay into a very thin sausage by rolling from side to side with a perspex square, as you would for a bail (see page 20), until it is 6 mm (¼) longer than the size required. Flatten the sausage slightly with the perspex square. Spilt the sausage in half at one end by 6 mm (¼ in) with a needle tool or cutter. Add a thin layer of water over the clay and let the water absorb completely. Smooth the cut edges with water.

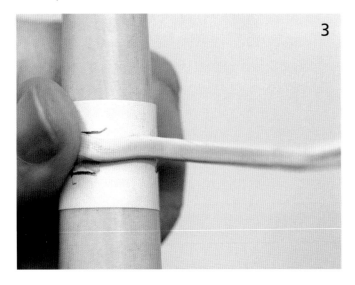

3 Using a paintbrush, apply a small dab of paste onto the paper on the mandrel, avoiding the place where the adhesive tape is. Attach one end of the sausage between the markings on the paper and turn the mandrel so it wraps around.

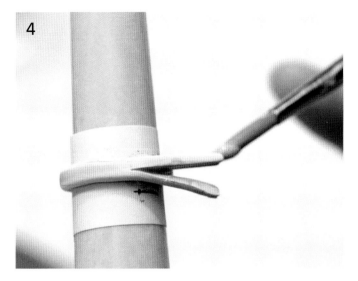

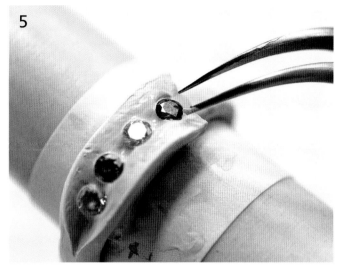

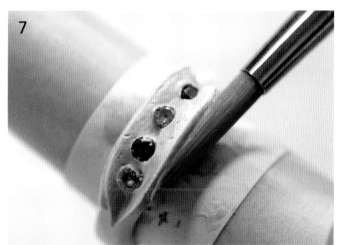

4 Where the coil starts to meet, apply a thick layer of paste to the underside, then press to split coil gently down with a damp brush to attach. Take care not to press too hard or the clay will go baggy on the underside.

5 Place the cubic zirconias into position using a pair of tweezers. If you are using two different colours, make sure you alternate them. Smooth the edges with the side of a brush.

6 Using a needle tool, press in the cubic zirconias between the split coils, making sure that the sides of the stones sit below the top of the clay.

7 Smooth out any distortion caused by pushing the stones in with the edge of a damp brush. Any small dents in the clay can be carefully smoothed out in the same manner.

8 Allow to dry thoroughly, then slide the paper off the mandrel and file and sand the clay. If necessary, fill any gaps with paste, then allow to dry again.

9 Fire in a kiln or with a blowtorch, according to the manufacturer's instructions. Remove the fire scale with a stainless steel brush and use a burnisher for a higher shine.

Tips

✿ Make sure you apply a thick layer of paste to the underside of the coil, otherwise the join can pull apart when firing.

✿ Be careful not to make the hole bigger when smoothing the inside of the ring.

Variation

Casting grains are great for decoration. They are available in fine silver and gold and tend to be irregular shapes, giving a slightly rough, organic effect to your jewellery.

Bracelet buttons

These silver clay buttons are fantastic to use with beads, cords and ribbons for many different designs. Here, Swarovski buttons have been used alternately with the silver buttons to make an eye-catching contrast of textures.

Skill level: **Beginner** ★

MATERIALS
- balm
- 25 g (1 oz) silver clay
- corrugated cardboard
- 4 Swarovski buttons
- 13 to18 jump rings (7 mm) depending on wrist size
- clasp

TOOLS
- work board
- spacer bars plus 4 playing cards or 12 playing cards
- acrylic roller
- circle cutters
- drill
- files
- sandpaper
- kiln or blowtorch
- stainless steel brush
- metal or agate burnisher
- jewellery pliers

to make the bracelet

1 Apply balm to your hands and roll the clay firmly in your palms. Place on a work board and put either two sets of six playing cards or two sets of spacer bars with two playing cards on both sides of the clay. Roll clay out using a roller.

2 Using your finger, apply a small amount of balm over the top of the clay.

3 Take a piece of cardboard and remove the top layer so that the corrugated layer is left. Place the cardboard over the clay and roll to leave an impression.

4 Pull back the corrugated cardboard gently. This will help to keep the ridges that you have created from distorting.

5 Cut four circle shapes out of the clay using circle cutters, then allow to dry.

6 Your buttons should all be the same size but the ridges will be slightly different.

7 Use a drill to make holes on either side of each circle, making sure that they line up.

Tips

❀ Lift the cardboard up slowly to see the pattern. If it is not deep enough, gently lower the cardboard and roll again.

❀ Place the cardboard on top of the acrylic spacer bars to make sure that the clay is not rolled too thin.

❀ Try to drill a hole in the bottom of the ridge or the smooth area on top as it is difficult to drill a hole in the side of a ridge.

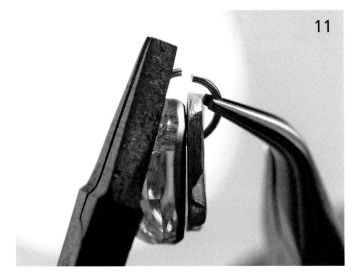

Tips

✿ When torch firing keep an eye on where the holes are drilled, in order to gauge temperature.

✿ Have a timer to hand.

✿ Do not try to torch fire with your lights on. A true colour cannot be seen to gauge the sintering process.

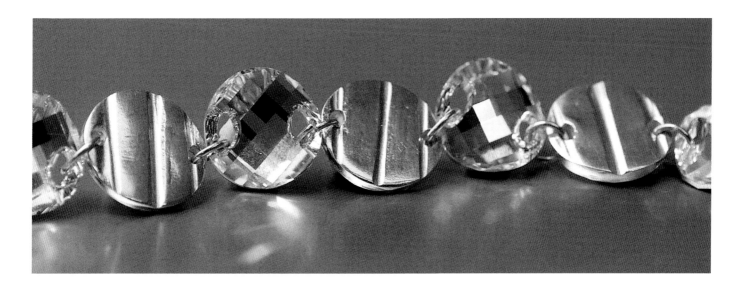

8 File and sand the pieces, then fire all together in a kiln or one piece at time with a blowtorch, according to the manufacturer's instructions.

9 Remove the fire scale with a stainless steel brush and use a burnisher to high shine the ridges.

10 If you would like to give your piece a more satin finish, use polishing papers instead of a burnisher.

11 Using jewellery pliers, link the silver buttons and the Swarovski buttons together alternately with jump rings (see page 29). Finish with a clasp on one end.

Variation

To make a drop necklace, simply cut a couple of clay discs, with the Swarovski button in the centre. Remember that one of the silver disks will only need one drill hole. Attach together with jump rings and run a chain through the top jump ring.

Ripple pendant

Create unusual shapes and textures with cardboard. Paper and leaves are other materials that make great paste projects. If you want you could add a little sparkle to these organic shapes by attaching cubic zirconias.

Skill level: **Beginner** ★

MATERIALS
- small piece of corrugated cardboard
- 15 g (½ oz) silver clay paste
- balm
- 9 g (¼ oz) silver clay
- 40–46 cm (16–18 in) silver chain, depending on desired length of necklace

TOOLS
- scissors
- paintbrush
- sandpaper
- kiln
- work board
- acrylic roller
- small perspex square or snake roller
- clay shaper
- straw
- files
- stainless steel brush
- metal or agate burnisher (optional)

to make the pendant

1 Remove the top layer of the cardboard to reveal its corrugated layer and cut out a small oval shape. With a slightly damp paintbrush apply a thin and even coat of paste onto the corrugated side. Allow to dry. This will be the front of the piece when fired.

2 Apply another thick layer of paste and allow to dry. Repeat this six to eight times until it is as thick as four playing cards, allowing each coat to dry before applying the next coat.

3 When dry, turn the piece over and sand any rough edges. Fire on a slow fire in kiln according to the manufacturer's instructions; the cardboard will burn away to leave a corrugated piece of silver.

4 Using the clay shaper and straw, make a looped bail (see page 20).

5 Using a paintbrush and plenty of paste, attach the bail to the pendant. Allow to dry.

6 When the bail is completely dry, file any rough edges with a file.

7 Use sandpaper to get to any awkward rough edges and to give a smoother finish to your bail.

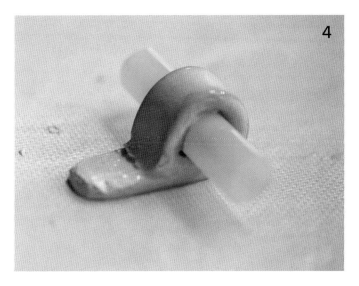

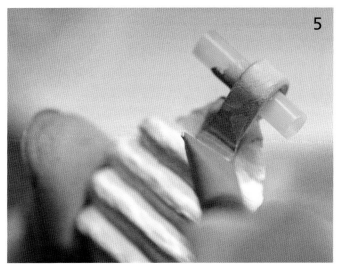

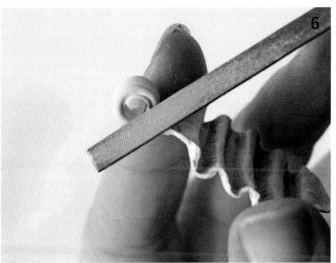

Tips

✿ Apply quite a thick layer of paste to the cardboard, otherwise you have to apply several layers, allowing for each to dry before applying the next one.

✿ Make sure that the paste goes right up to the edges so that the sides of the piece are not fragile.

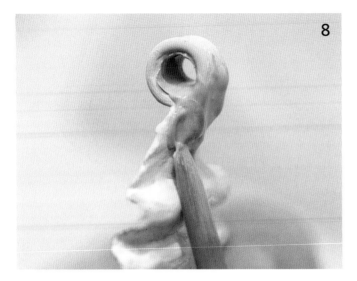

8 File and fill any gaps with paste. If paste is applied, allow to dry before firing again in the kiln.

9 Remove the fire scale with a stainless steel brush, then burnish with a metal or agate burnisher if a high shine is desired. String onto a silver chain to finish.

Tip

✿ Make sure you apply plenty of coats of paste – otherwise the structure will be too weak and will break, even after firing.

Variation

This variation on the pendant has been made in the same way but has had syringe decoration added and cubic zirconias pressed into it.

Curved heart bracelet

Capture the fingerprints of your loved ones in this pretty bracelet design. The liver of sulphur can be applied to the hearts as many times as you like to achieve the desired shade. This piece has a satin finish but you could also give it a high shine if you prefer.

MATERIALS
- balm
- 34 g (1¼ oz) silver clay
- silver clay paste
- liquid detergent or bicarbonate of soda
- liver of sulphur
- 24 x 6 mm jump rings
- 17 x 4 mm jump rings
- clasp

TOOLS
- work board
- spacer bars or 8 playing cards
- acrylic roller or perspex square
- rectangle cutter
- small heart cutter
- 6 light bulbs
- 2 paintbrushes
- files
- sandpaper
- drill
- kiln pillow
- kiln or blowtorch
- stainless steel brush
- metal or agate burnisher (optional)
- glass jar
- jewellery pliers

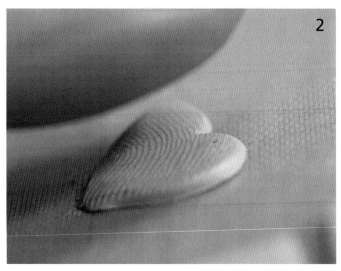

Tips

✿ Thoroughly wash hands before applying a fingerprint so
that any balm or grease doesn't mask the ridges and no dirt
is embedded into the clay.

✿ You don't need to wait for the hearts to dry before attaching
to the rectangles – just make sure you don't distort the shape
of the heart or the fingerprint pattern.

to make the bracelet

1 Apply balm to hands, then roll clay firmly in palms of hands. Place on work board, put spacer bars or four playing cards on either side of the clay and roll firmly with a roller or perspex square. Cut out six rectangle shapes using the rectangle cutter, re-rolling the trimmings if necessary. Out of three of these rectangles, cut three small hearts with the heart cutter.

2 Press a finger into the three heart shapes to leave an impression.

3 Place the rectangles on light bulbs to create curved shapes. Allow to dry.

4 Using a paintbrush, apply a thick layer of paste to the back of the small hearts.

5 Attach the small hearts onto the three rectangles without the heart-shaped holes. Clean up any excess paste and fill any gaps around the edges of the hearts with a damp brush. Allow to dry.

6 Sand to give a smooth finish on the rectangles, then drill holes in the corners of each of the six rectangles.

7 File the edges of the rectangles. The easiest way to do this without distorting the shape is to place a piece of sandpaper on your work board and move the rectangle shape back and forth over it.

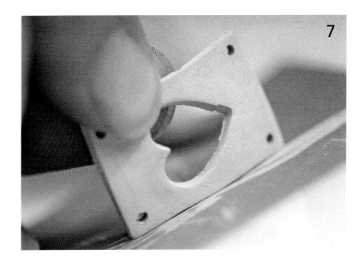

▷

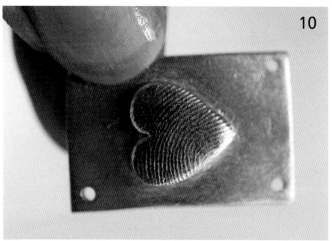

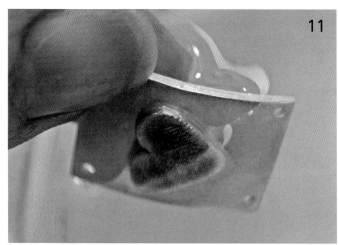

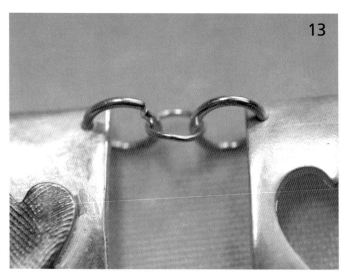

8 Fire the pieces all together on a kiln pillow in kiln or fire each rectangle separately with a blowtorch according to the manufacturer's instructions. Remove the fire scale with a stainless steel brush and use a burnisher if a high shine is required.

9 Wash the silver pieces with liquid detergent or bicarbonate of soda to remove any dirt or grease. Add a few drops of liver of sulphur to a jar of hot water. Apply with a paintbrush to the small hearts.

10 You will start to see the effects of the liver of sulphur straight away.

11 Rinse the pieces in cold water. then repeat the application of liver of sulphur and rinsing until the hearts are as dark as you want them. Give a final good rinse in cold water to stop the colour becoming too dark.

12 Attach the larger jump rings to each corner of the rectangles using jewellery pliers (see page 29).

Variation

Use much smaller cutters to create matching earrings. Simply drill a hole in the rectangle and use earring wires. Alternatively you can attach eyelets and attach earring wires to those.

13 Then join the rectangles together by linking the larger jump rings with the smaller ones. Finally, attach the clasp onto one of the end jump rings.

Daisy bracelet

This summery bracelet is made from pretty curved flowers, decorated with gemstones and joined together with a silver bracelet chain fed through bridge bails. For a slightly more random look, use cubic zirconias in an assortment of colours.

Skill level: **Intermediate** ★★

MATERIALS

- balm
- 16 g (½ oz) silver clay
- silver clay paste
- silver clay syringe
- 7 x 3 or 4 mm (⅛ or ⅙ in) cubic zirconias
- 165 cm (5½ ft) of 22-gauge fine silver wire
- 34 x 6 mm (¼ in) top-drilled Swarovski crystals AB
- 18–20 cm (7–8 in) silver bracelet chain

TOOLS

- work board
- spacer bars or 8 playing cards
- acrylic roller
- snake roller or perspex square
- daisy cutter
- 7 marbles
- Blu-Tack or White Tack
- paintbrush
- tweezers
- straw
- files
- sandpaper
- blowtorch
- kiln (optional)
- stainless steel brush
- tumbler (optional)
- metal or agate burnisher
- wire cutters
- solder tweezers
- round nose pliers

to make the bracelet

1 Apply balm to hands and firmly roll the clay between the palms of your hands. Place clay on work board, put spacer bars or 4 playing cards on either side and roll out firmly using a roller or perspex square. Using cutters, cut out seven daisy shapes. (You will have to re-roll the clay to get the last two daisy shapes cut out.) Wrap the remaining clay in some plastic and seal in the clay packet. You will need this later for the bails.

2 Secure the marbles into Blu-Tack or White Tack and apply a small amount of balm to each one. Carefully lay the daisy shapes over the marbles using a paintbrush and allow to dry.

3 Remove the daisies from the marbles and apply a dab of paste to the centre of each.

Tips

❀ A 25 g (1 oz) packet will give you enough clay to make earrings or a drop necklace to go with the bracelet.

❀ If you want to create a slightly bigger hole for your doughnut shapes, simply trim the end of the syringe tip with some sharp scissors.

4 Syringe a ring of clay, three layers deep, on top of the paste on each daisy. There needs to be enough depth to hold a 4 mm (⅙ in) cubic zirconia.

5 Using tweezers, press in a cubic zirconia onto each daisy. Allow to dry. When dry, check the stone is attached to the flower. If there are any gaps, fill with paste and re-dry.

6 Make 7 bridge bails and attach using paste (see page 21), making sure the hole in the bail is big enough for the bracelet chain to pass through. Dry thoroughly.

7 File and sand any rough edges. Fire the shapes all together in a kiln or individually with blowtorch according to the manufacturer's instructions.

8 Use a stainless steel brush to remove the fire scale. If you have a tumbler, burnish with this, then burnish with a metal or agate burnisher for a high shine.

9 Cut a 5 cm (2 in) piece of wire and ball one end using a blowtorch (see page 29). Thread a crystal onto the wire, then ball the other end, keeping the crystal at the end of the wire that is not being heated. Using the round nose pliers, form a circular shape with the wire and twist the ends together, then tuck the two ends downwards. Repeat this process with each of the remaining 33 crystals.

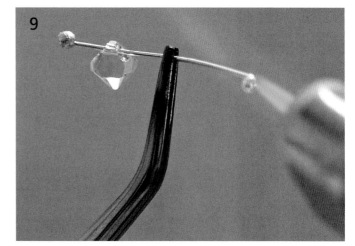

10 Thread the loops of five of the crystals onto the bracelet chain, then thread on a daisy. Thread on three more crystals and a daisy and repeat this pattern to the end, adding five crystals on the very end. Squeeze the wire firmly together under the chain of the first and last crystal; this is will act as a stopper bead on the bracelet.

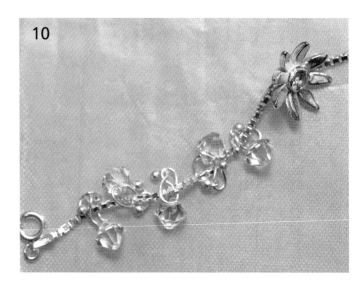

Variation

This variation shows a daisy necklace. It has one daisy shape placed on top of another, creating a space in the middle to run a chain or ribbon through. This could also be made into earrings by attaching eyelets and using earring wires.

$\mathcal{P}$endant with dichroic glass

The vibrant dichroic glass beautifully complements the textured silver in this striking pendant. You can find lovely dichroic glass in a range of colours, ranging from opaque opals to sparkling glass.

Skill level: **intermediate** ★ ★

MATERIALS
- balm
- 9 g (¼ oz) silver clay
- silver clay paste
- 1 small circular piece of dichroic glass
- silver clay syringe
- 40–46 cm (16–18 in) ribbon or cord, depending on desired length
- 2 silver cord endings
- 3 x 5 mm jump rings
- clasp

TOOLS
- work board
- spacer bars or 8 playing cards
- acrylic roller
- texture mat
- shape cutter
- needle tool
- paintbrush
- drill

- files
- sandpaper
- kiln
- stainless steel brush
- metal or agate burnisher
- jewellery pliers

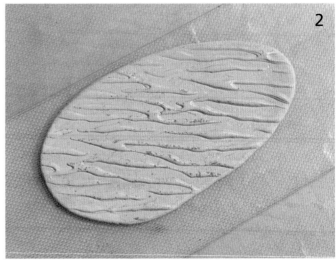

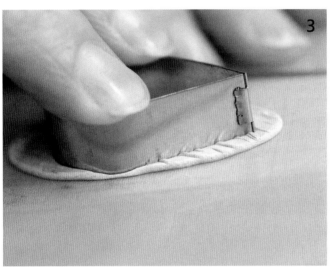

Tips

✿ Make sure the paste around the hole edge is thick enough so that it doesn't dry out too quickly.

✿ If you have got paint on the glass let it dry before you try to remove it.

✿ Make sure the glass is clean and free of fingerprints before firing or they will show in the glass.

to make the pendant

1 Apply balm to your hands and give the clay a firm roll between the palms of your hands. Place on a work board, put spacer bars or cards on either side and roll firmly.

2 Apply a small amount of balm to the top of the clay and gently work over the surface, then place a texture mat on top and gently roll over to leave an impression in the clay.

3 Cut a shape out of the clay with a cutter, taking care not to smudge the texture.

4 Carefully peel away the excess clay, leaving a perfect teardrop shape.

5 Using a needle tool, cut a hole slightly smaller than the piece of glass. Apply a thick layer of paste around the hole with a paintbrush so that the edge of the paste is slightly bigger than the glass shape.

6 Press the glass firmly down over the hole on top of the paste.

7 Syringe a ring of clay around the glass shape (without the syringe cap on). Allow to dry, then fill in any gaps between the syringed clay and the clay base.

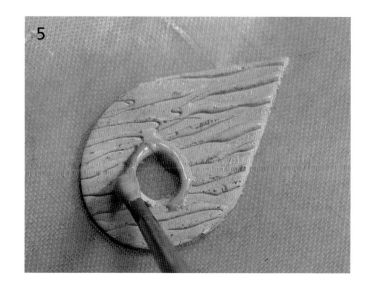

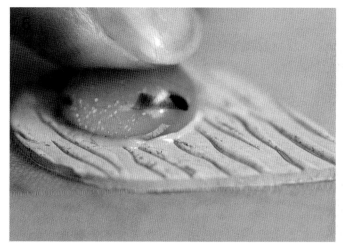

8 Dry thoroughly, then drill a hole in the clay pendant, taking care not to drill too close to the tip. Don't apply too much pressure when turning the drill.

9 Smooth away any rough edges with a file or some sandpaper. Fire on a slow fire in kiln according to the manufacturer's instructions. Allow the glass to cool slowly in the kiln or it can lead to thermal shock in the glass.

10 Use a stainless steel brush to remove the fire scale and burnish with a metal or agate burnisher. Thread the ribbon or cord through the hole and attach cord endings. Finally, attach jump rings and a clasp using jewellery pliers (see page 29).

Variation

This necklace has a looped bail added and a hole drilled in both
pieces which are then joined together with a jump ring.

$\mathcal{H}$eavenly angel necklace

These adorable little angels are created by making a mould from moulding compound. You can customize them with cubic zirconias, engraved names and many other materials. You can make your own moulds from a number of objects such as sea shells or fossils.

Skill level: **Intermediate** ★★

MATERIALS
- small piece of thick card
- two-part moulding compound
- 9 g (¼ oz) silver clay
- a few cubic zirconias (2–3 mm)
- eyelet
- silver clay paste

TOOLS
- angel craft punch
- acrylic roller
- needle tool
- paintbrush
- pencil
- carving tool

- files
- sandpaper
- kiln or blowtorch
- stainless steel brush
- metal or agate burnisher (optional)

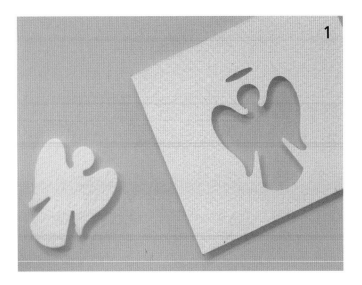

to make the necklace

1 Using thick card, cut an angel shape using a craft punch.

2 Mix a small amount of the two-part moulding compound together and roller over lightly to form an even surface. Press the cardboard angel firmly into the moulding compound and allow it to harden to form a mould.

3 Use the acrylic roller to flatten the clay slightly. Remove the cardboard angel, then press the clay into the mould. After a few minutes, press out the clay while it is still damp.

4 Use a needle tool to remove the excess clay, then smooth the rough edges with a damp paintbrush.

5 Press in a cubic zirconia with the tip of the needle tool, making sure the stones are pushed in just below the surface of the clay. This is to ensure that the stones do not pop out when the clay shrinks on being fired. Allow to dry.

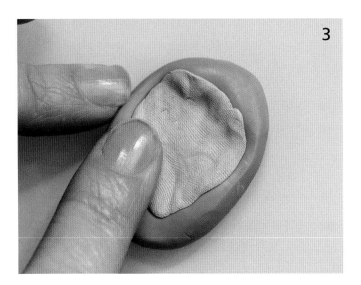

6 Do not feel that you have to use the cubic zirconias in the same pattern as shown here. Arrange your stones in any way you choose.

7 When the clay is dry use a pencil to draw lines on the angel.

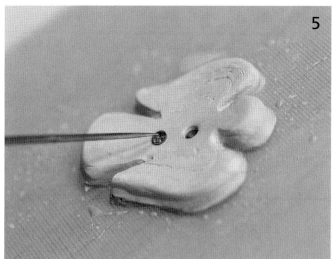

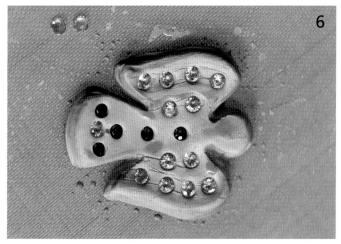

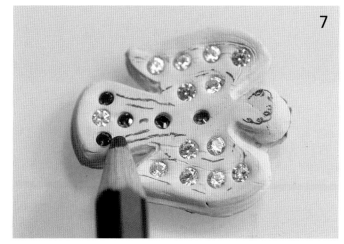

Tips

❀ If you want to use bigger stones than the ones listed you will need to syringe a doughnut shape onto the clay base to push the stones into.

❀ Make sure the cubic zirconias are free from dust before firing.

❀ Cotton buds are very handy for cleaning stones.

8 Use a carving tool to carve out the design, following your pencil lines. Remove the dried shavings with a dry paintbrush.

9 Attach the eyelet with a good blob of paste. Allow to dry and fire in a kiln or with a blowtorch according to the manufacturer's instructions.

10 Use a stainless steel brush to remove the fire scale and burnish with a metal or agate burnisher if required.

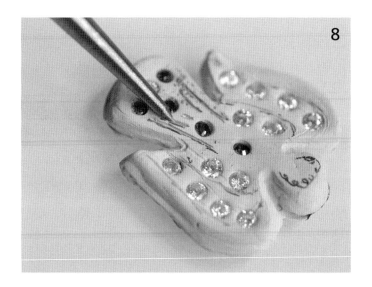

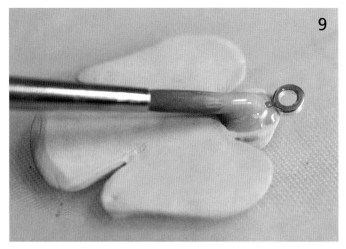

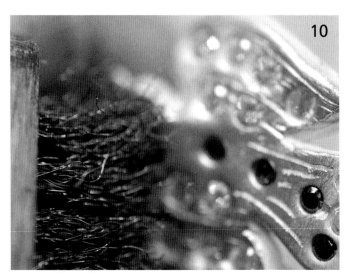

Variation

This angel has had a big 5 mm heart positioned in the centre. To do this you will need to remove a plug of clay. Add paste around the hole and syringe a shape on top. Push the stone in just below the clay surface.

Resin anemone brooch

This pretty flower is brought to life with the use of layers of colourful resin. The instructions below are for UV resin; if using epoxy resin please refer to the manufacturer's instructions.

Skill level: **Intermediate** ★★

MATERIALS
- 16 g (½ oz) silver clay
- silver clay paste
- 4 mm cubic zirconia
- brooch backs and pin
- UV resin or two-part epoxy resin
- acrylic colours

TOOLS
- balm
- work board
- spacer bars or 8 playing cards
- texture mat
- acrylic roller
- anemone cutter
- small circle cutter
- small straw
- paintbrush
- needle tool
- large spoon or other curved object
- files
- sandpaper
- kiln or blowtorch
- stainless steel brush
- metal or agate burnisher (optional)
- baking parchment paper or tile for mixing colours
- measuring cups (for two-part epoxy resin only)
- cocktail sticks
- UV light box (for UV resin only)
- fume mask (for epoxy resin only)
- jewellery pliers

to make the brooch

1 Balm your hands and roll the clay firmly in your palms. Place the clay on a work board with spacer bars or four cards on either side. Apply a small amount of balm over the surface of the clay, then place a texture mat on top and roll lightly over the clay with a roller or perspex square to leave an impression.

2 Cut out an anemone shape and a small circle shape using the cutters.

3 Use a small straw to remove a plug of clay from the centre of the circle by making a small twisting motion.

4 Add a small dab of paste onto the centre of the anemone shape and attach the small circle.

5 Use a needle tool to press in a cubic zirconia, making sure that it is set slightly lower than the surface of the clay.

6 Lightly balm a spoon or other curved object, then dry the anemone in the spoon to give it a curved shape. When dry, file and sand any rough edges.

7 Attach the brooch backs with paste. Dry, then fire in a kiln or with torch according to the manufacturer's instructions. Remove the fire scale with a stainless steel brush and burnish if required with a metal or agate burnisher.

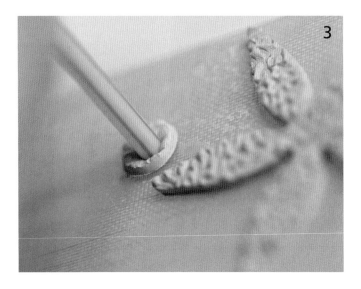

Tips

❀ If using UV resin, line the bottom of the UV box with aluminium foil, it will help reflect the light.

❀ Do not mix too much colour pigment into UV gel as it can stop the curing process; it is better to build the depth of colour by adding more layers.

❀ If the UV resin feels slightly sticky, just add a clear coat of gel to seal, and cure.

▷

8 Wash the silver piece to remove any dirt and dry. Then mix the UV resin with the colourants (you only need a very small amount of colour).

9 Apply a thin layer of resin to the silver piece, then cure under a UV lamp for 3 to 5 minutes if using UV resin. To avoid getting sticky fingers, apply resin to one half of the piece, cure and then do the other side.

10 Repeat until the required colour and tone is reached, curing it between each layer.

11 Attach the brooch bar pin into the brooch backs on the back of silver piece using jewellery pliers. Make sure you have both ends of the brooch pin in line with each other or the pin will not close properly.

Variation

Here a texture mat has been used and then small elements of the pattern colour with resin. A bridge back bail has been used on this piece so as not to interfere with the shape.

Silver barrel necklace

Simple but very effective, this barrel necklace uses the syringe technique. A simple bead has been decorated with a random syringed pattern but you could also add cubic zirconias and casting grains. A feature bead like this would look great on a cord or ribbon.

Skill level: **Intermediate** ★★

MATERIALS
- small square of paper
- white craft glue
- balm
- 16 g (½ oz) silver clay
- silver clay paste
- silver clay syringe

TOOLS
- work board
- spacer bars or 8 playing cards
- acrylic roller
- 2 paintbrushes
- 2 pipe cleaners
- oasis (flower arranging block)
- kiln pillow
- kiln
- metal file
- stainless steel brush
- agate burnisher or tumbler

to make the pendant

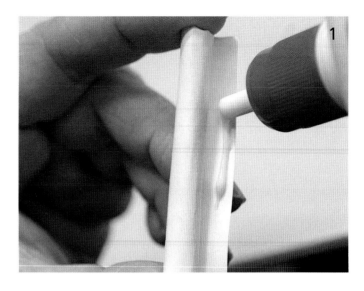

1 Roll the paper and glue the edge to make a cigar shape. Allow the glue to dry.

2 Balm your hands and roll the clay firmly in your palms, then place on a work board with spacer bars or four playing cards placed on either side. Roll out the clay.

3 Put a dab of paste onto the paper and attach one side of your clay to it.

Tip

 When the clay is dry check the seam of the lump clay where it joins to make sure there are no gaps and it will not fall apart on firing.

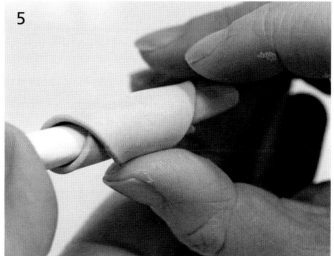

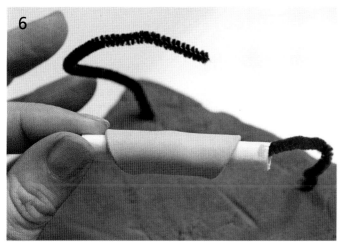

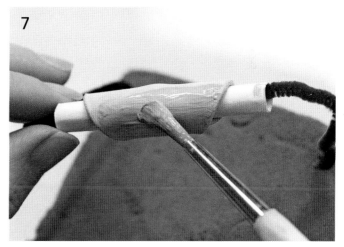

4 Hold the clay against the paper for a few moments before removing your finger. This will hold the clay in place so you can roll the shape without it falling off.

5 Roll the clay over the paper and attach the join with a thick layer of paste painted onto the underside. Press your finger lightly down over join and hold for a few minutes. Take care not to apply too much pressure or the barrel shape will go slightly baggy around the paper.

6 Insert a pipe cleaner into each end and then push the ends of the pipe cleaners into a block of oasis.

7 When the bead is dry, use a paintbrush to coat the bead with a layer of paste.

▷

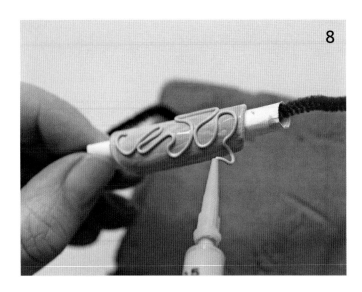

8 While the paste is still wet, syringe a pattern over the top.

9 Flatten the syringed pattern slightly with edge of a damp brush to make sure it is fully attached to the barrel. Allow to dry.

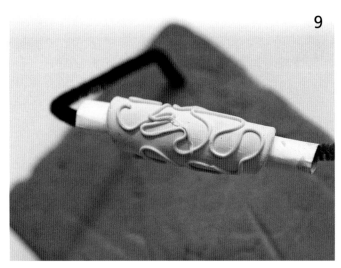

Tip

❀ When adding a layer of paste to the syringed barrel to secure on the syringed pattern, it is much easier to cover the entire barrel and syringe with paste than trying to follow the syringe line, because this would look patchy and then require sanding between the syringe lines.

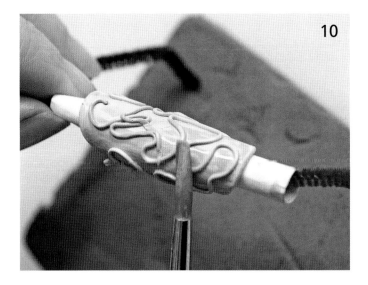

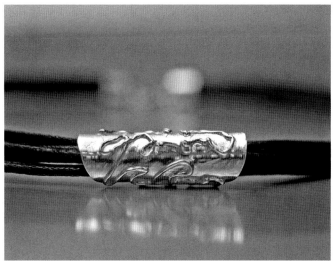

Variation

Decorate the barrel with cubic zirconias to add extra sparkle. To do this syringe doughnut shapes onto the barrel, making sure they are deep enough to press a cubic zirconia into.

10 When dry, run a thin coat of paste over entire bead, making sure the edges of the syringe are well attached to the barrel bead with no gaps. Dry thoroughly.

11 Place on a kiln pillow in the kiln. Do not remove paper and fire according to the manufacturer's instructions. File the silver barrel edges if rough and use a stainless steel brush to remove the fire scale. Highlight the syringed areas with an agate burnisher or place in a tumbler if you have one.

Snowflake pendant

This pretty pendant is made up of four smaller snowflakes joined together with paste and decorated with a crystal for extra winter sparkle. If you wish, you can leave a little of the fire scale on around the centre to create a snowy effect.

Skill level: **Advanced** ★★

MATERIALS
- balm
- 25 g (1 oz) lump clay
- silver clay paste
- syringe
- 5 mm cubic zirconia

TOOLS
- balm
- work board
- spacer bars or 8 playing cards
- acrylic roller
- texture mat
- snowflake cutter, 2.5 cm (1 in) from tip to tip
- 13 mm (½ in) small circle cutter
- paintbrush
- straw
- needle tool
- perspex square or snake roller
- kiln
- stainless steel brush
- metal or agate burnisher (optional)

to make the pendant

1 Balm your hands and roll the clay firmly in the palms of your hands. Place on a work board and put spacer bars or four cards on either side of the clay. Roll the clay out firmly with a roller, then apply a small amount of balm to the surface of the clay. Place a texture mat on top of the clay and roll lightly across the surface to leave a slight impression in the clay.

2 Cut out four snowflake shapes and a circle. If clay gets stuck in the cutter, push out very gently with the side of a damp paintbrush. You may need to re-roll the clay to cut out the fourth snowflake shape.

3 Use a straw to remove a plug of clay with straw from the circle. To do this twist the straw slightly and pull out.

4 Paint a thin layer of paste around the hole and then syringe a doughnut shape on top.

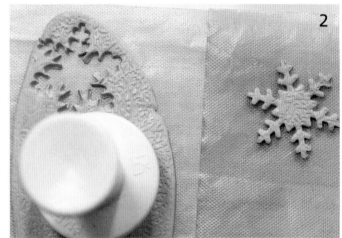

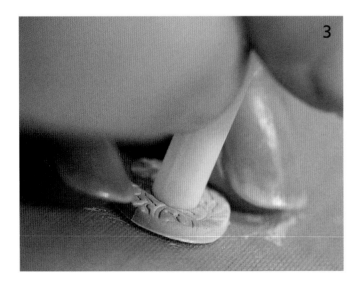

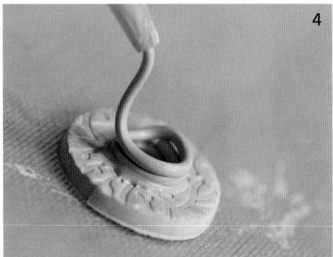

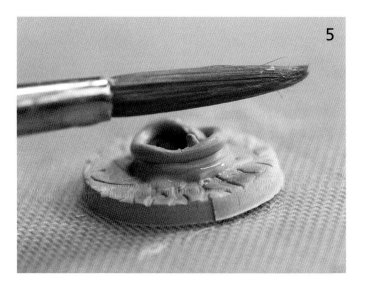

5 To even up the top of your doughnut, use a damp paintbrush and gently touch the doughnut using the edge of your brush.

6 Use a needle tool to push a cubic zirconia into the clay; it must sit slightly lower than the top of the syringe doughnut to allow for the shrinkage of the clay. Allow to dry.

7 Meanwhile, make a bridge bail and attach to the back of one of the snowflakes with paste (see page 21). Dry thoroughly.

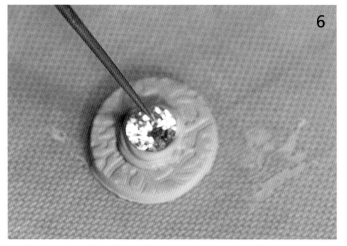

Tips

❀ When syringing the doughnut shape on the circle make sure it has enough depth for a 5 mm stone to be set into.

❀ You will only need a small amount of clay for the bridge bail as it needs to be narrow enough to fit on the tip of the snowflake.

8 Arrange the snowflakes, textured-side down, on a perspex square so that the tips are touching, creating one large snowflake. This will allow you to view the arrangement from underneath. Apply a dab of paste to the inside edge of the snowflake tips to join them together.

9 Apply paste to the circle around the edge of the stone, then place, stone-side down, onto the snowflake tips and press slightly down. Check it is in the correct position by lifting up the perspex square to view it from underneath. Allow to dry.

10 To make the structure more sound, apply a couple of layers of paste to the tips of the snowflakes and apply paste to where the snowflakes meet the circle; this will really strengthen the whole piece. Allow to dry.

11 Fire in a kiln according to the manufacturer's instructions. Remove the fire scale with a stainless steel brush and burnish with a metal or agate burnisher if required.

Variation

This variation shows a snowflake that has had eyelets pasted onto the bottom tips and one on the top to hang an earring wire on. Teardrop shapes have been added with jump rings.

Shooting stars necklace

This impressive piece uses thin strips of wire to
hold together silver gem-embedded stars and a
half moon. The project involves delicate work so
wait until you are completely confident using
metal clay before tackling it. Fine silver wire will
not take on the black oxidization that happens
with sterling silver.

Skill level: **Advanced** ★ ★ ★

MATERIALS
- balm
- 25 g (1 oz) silver clay
- at least 24 cm (10 in) of 20-gauge fine silver wire
- 4 x 3 mm (⅛ in) cubic zirconias
- silver clay paste
- 40–46 cm (16–18 in) silver chain, depending on desired length of necklace

TOOLS
- work board
- spacer bars plus 4 playing cards or 12 playing cards
- acrylic roller
- snake roller or perspex square
- texture mat
- medium star cutter
- small star cutter
- circle cutter
- wire cutters
- jewellery pliers
- needle tool
- paintbrush
- straw
- files
- sandpaper
- kiln or blowtorch
- stainless steel brush
- metal or agate burnisher

to make the necklace

1 Balm your hands and firmly roll the clay in your palms. Place on a work board, put either a spacer bar plus two cards or six playing cards on both sides of the clay and roll out using a roller or perspex square. Place a texture mat on top of the clay and roll lightly across the surface to leave an impression in the clay.

2 Cut one medium star plus three small star shapes out of the clay using the star cutters. Use a circle cutter to cut out a half moon shape.

3 Remove the stars from the clay before you cut your half moon shape, as they will be cut quite close together.

4 Cut 3 strips of silver wire 8 cm (3 in) long using wire cutters. Flatten one end of each wire using pliers and insert each into one of the three small stars.

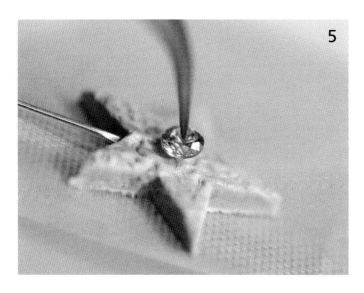

5 Press cubic zirconias into the front of all the star shapes with a needle tool, making sure that they sit slightly lower than clay surface. Allow to dry.

6 You will only need to insert the wire into the small star shapes.

7 Remove excess clay from packet, roll out a thin section, only a couple of cards deep, and cut out another star using the small star cutter and a half moon shape using the circle cutter.

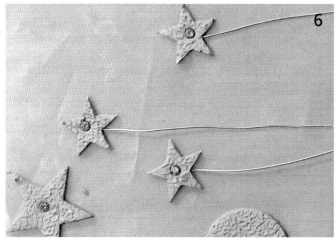

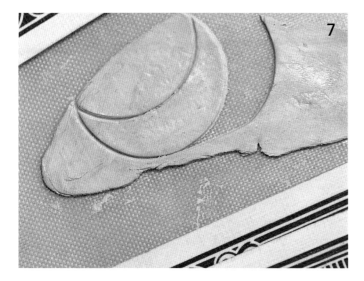

Tip

✿ Allow to cool naturally; never quench pieces with cubic zirconias set in or they will fracture.

✿ If you get paste on the fine silver wire do not worry – it is easy to file afterwards with some sandpaper.

▷

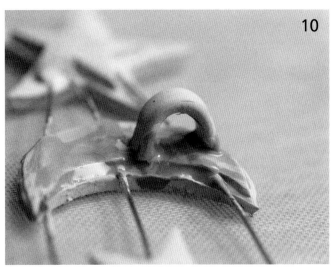

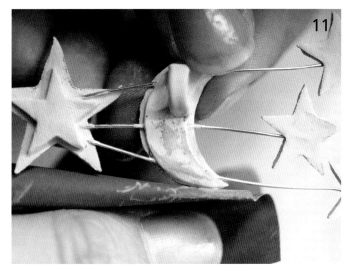

Tips

✿ Site your bail at the top of the moon or the weight of it will make the piece flop forward when wearing.

✿ Have your small stars placed at slightly different lengths to avoid them fighting for space while working on them.

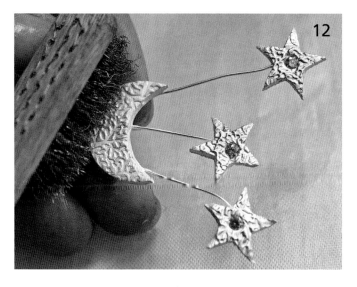

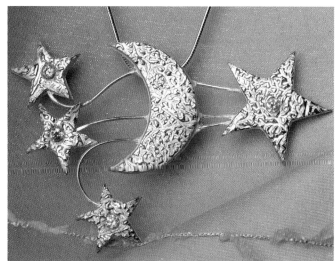

8 Paste the back area on both the dry, textured moon and the medium star. Then lay the silver wires across the paste so that they go over the moon and converge on the medium star. Trim the wires if necessary so that are the same length. Allow to dry.

9 Apply paste onto the extra small star and moon shape and attach over the wires on the back of the medium star and the moon. Allow to dry.

10 Make a bridge bail and attach it to the moon using paste (see page 21). Allow to dry and file any rough edges.

11 File the edges with sandpaper to remove any roughness. Any paste on the wires can also be sanded away.

12 Fire all together in a kiln or individually with a blowtorch according to the manufacturer's instructions, with wires facing upwards. Remove the fire scale with a stainless steel brush and use a burnisher for higher shine if required. Thread through a silver chain to finish.

Variation

This could easily be turned into a brooch – simply site a brooch pin so that it is running from the large star to the moon.

Enamelled pendant

Enamels give a beautifully coloured high-gloss finish. When choosing enamels, be aware that certain colours fire at different rates; the blue colour spectrum is the easiest to fire as they have a similar firing schedule.

Skill level: **Advanced** ★★★

MATERIALS
- balm
- 9 g (¼ oz) silver clay
- silver clay paste
- silver clay syringe
- eyelet
- enamels
- distilled water

TOOLS
- spacer bars plus 4 playing cards or 12 playing cards
- acrylic roller
- shaped cutter
- 2 paintbrushes
- files or sandpaper
- kiln
- blowtorch (optional)
- glass brush or wire brush and pumice powder
- safety goggles
- pestle and mortar
- cloth
- glass jars or clear plastic containers with lids
- straw
- scissors
- heatproof gloves
- metal mesh
- kiln tongs
- solder tweezers
- stainless steel or brass brush
- metal or agate burnisher (optional)

Tips

✿ If you use circular or domed shapes make them at least
1.3 mm (½ in) deep and you will not need to use a counter-
enamel on the back.

✿ Powdered enamels are the easiest to use but I often regrind
mine in a pestle and mortar for a smoother finish.

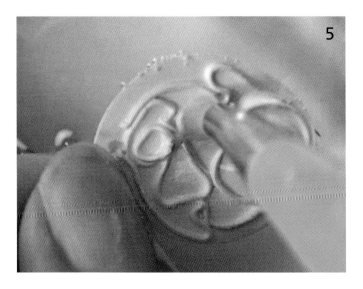

to make the pendant

1 Balm hands and roll clay firmly in the palms of your hands. Place a spacer bar plus two cards or six playing cards on both sides of the clay and roll out using a roller. Cut the shape for the pendant with a cutter and allow to dry.

2 Apply an even layer of paste to the top, then syringe on a pattern. Flatten the clay slightly with the edge of damp brush to make sure syringed pattern is fully attached, then allow to dry. Once dry, use a file or sandpaper to remove any rough edges.

3 Apply a blob of paste to the back of the piece and attach the eyelet.

4 Make sure you have added enough paste to your eyelet for it to be secure. Dry and fire in a in a kiln or with a blowtorch, according to the manufacturer's instructions.

5 Clean the fired silver piece with a glass brush or a wire brush and pumice under running water, then leave to dry. Once you have cleaned your silver avoid touching the surface that is to be enamelled. Otherwise you will transmit oils from your hands which can interfere withe the enamelling process.

6 Put on your safety goggles when you start using the enamels. Place one of your chosen enamel colours in pestle and mortar and pour a little water over to cover the enamel. Place a cloth over the top and grind. Place the enamel powder into a cup or jar and pour distilled water onto the powder. Tap the side of your jar and allow to settle for a few seconds, then pour the cloudy water away and repeat until the water is clear. Then put into a container with a lid. Repeat with all the colours.

▷

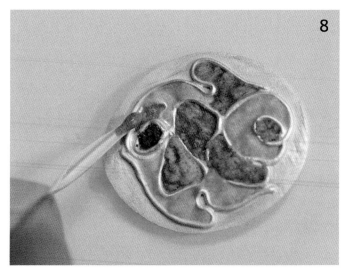

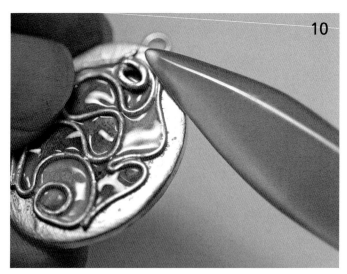

7 Once the enamels are ready for use, cut a diagonal section out from the straw with scissors. It should be in a shovel shape.

8 Apply the enamels using a straw, or if you prefer, you can use a clean paintbrush. Allow to dry.

9 Before firing you will need to put on heatproof gloves. Place the dried enamel on a wire mesh and transfer this to a kiln. Use kiln tongs to place the

wire mesh in the kiln, then fire in a kiln at a temperature around 850+°C (1560+°F) for approximately 30 to 90 seconds until it looks like crystallized sugar, then repeat the process until the enamel has a glossy finish. Use solder tweezers to remove the piece from the wire mesh.

10 Use a stainless steel or brass brush on any silver showing, followed with burnisher if required.

Variation

A deep relief texture mat could be used with interesting effect. Lay the enamels into the recessed areas on the silver, building up the colours as desired.

Flower bud brooch

Using both sheet clay and lump clay combined can give you such different textures with stunning results. Petal shapes are twisted together with wire to create this elegant brooch. Very intricate shapes can be cut from sheet clay and even when fired the silver clay can easily be manipulated.

Skill level: **Advanced** ★★★

MATERIALS
- 6 x 6 cm (2¼ x 2¼ x in) sheet of silver clay
- white craft glue
- 2 x 8 cm (3 in) lengths of 20-gauge fine silver wire
- balm
- 9 g (¼ oz) silver clay
- silver clay paste
- brooch backs and pin

TOOLS
- ruler
- pencil
- scissors
- 2 paintbrushes
- kiln or blowtorch
- wire cutter
- work board
- spacer bars or 8 playing cards
- acrylic roller
- heart cutter
- needle tool
- stainless steel brush
- polishing papers

to make the pendant

1 Take the square sheet of silver clay and cut off a 5 mm (¼ in) wide strip. Divide the remaining sheet into 8 equal sections and draw a petal in each section.

2 Cut out the petal shapes with scissors. Paste a little craft glue onto the base of two of the petals using a paintbrush and fold. Wait for the glue to dry, then fire the two petals together in a kiln or individually with a blowtorch according to the manufacturer's instructions.

3 When the petals are cool, use your fingers to wrap a piece of wire 8 cm (3 in) long around the base of each petal.

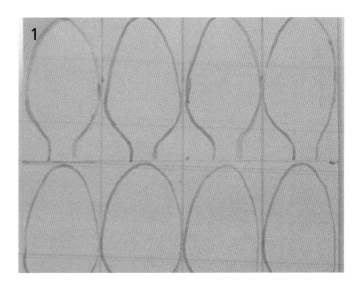

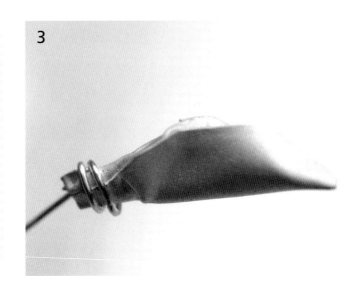

Tips

❁ Until the sheet is fired, do not apply water or paste as it will disintegrate. When fired, you can treat it as silver and any re-firing paste can be used.

❁ Do not try to wrap wire around unfired sheet clay as it will just rip.

4 Apply a small amount of glue to the base of the other petals and fold in the same way. On the odd petal, paste glue along with side of the petal and twist to create a curled petal.

5 Take four of the petals and assemble into a flower by glueing two on either side of one of the fired petals. Take the remaining two petals and glue them either side of the other fired petal. Allow the glue to dry. You should end up with one flower made up of five petals and one flower made up of three petals.

6 Cut the thin strip of sheet clay in half. Dab the wire and petal joins on the flowers with a little glue.

7 Wrap one strip of sheet clay around each flower. Allow to dry and then fire both flowers in a kiln or with a blowtorch, according to the manufacturer's instructions.

▷

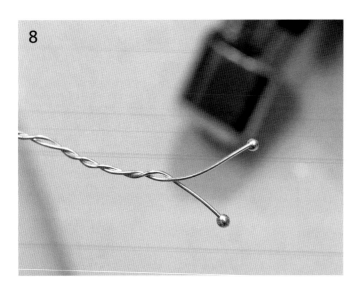

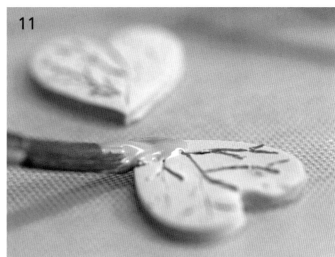

Tips

✿ If your wires are slightly too long, trim them before you ball the ends.

✿ Polishing papers are easier to use than a brush if you need to get right into the crevices.

8 Ball the ends of the wires with a blowtorch (see page 29), then twist the two wires together with your fingers to join the flower buds, taking care not to snap the wire.

9 Balm your hands and roll the lump clay firmly between the palms of your hands. Place on a work board, put a spacer bar or four cards on either side and roll out. Cut out two heart shapes using a heart cutter.

10 Using a needle tool, mark out some veins on the leaves.

11 Apply paste to the top of the heart at the pointed end, then place the twisted wire across the paste. Apply a thick blob of paste onto the wire and some paste to the underside of the second heart. Place the heart over the wire and press down. Allow to dry, then fill any gaps showing between the wire and the leaves.

12 Use paste to attach the brooch backs onto the heart leaves. Allow to dry, then fire again. Assemble the brooch pin, then brush with a stainless steel brush and polish with polishing papers.

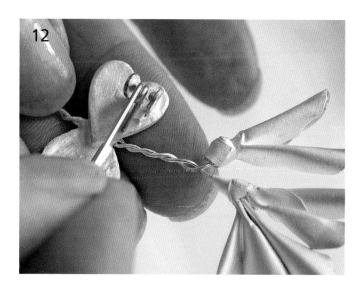

Variation

Thin strips of sheet clay can be woven together and fired to produce an interesting effect.

Galleries

Geraldine Mallinson

This wonderful collection of items by Geraldine Mallinson showcases a number of different techniques and materials, including clay paste, cork clay, liver of sulphur, enamel and lump clay.

Paula Louise Paton

These items are all made by Paula Louise Paton, who runs Precious Metal Clay jewellery courses and supplies materials. They show what a wonderful range of designs and effects can be achieved, from flower and leaf shapes to contemporary beads and multi-layered designs.

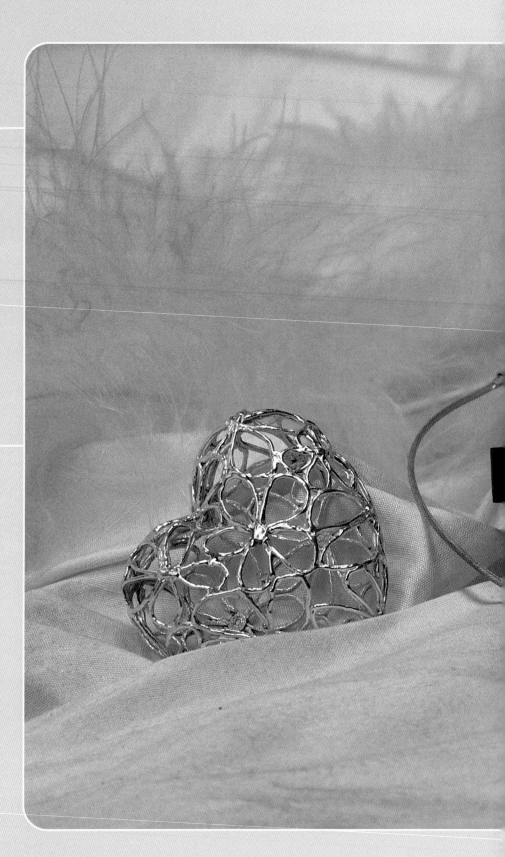

Jo Dix

Jo Dix runs courses and sells jewellery online. These lovely pieces include hollow hearts made with cork clay, a ring made with dichroic glass and a ring made with cubic zirconias and liver of sulphur.

Various

This collection of items shows the magic and versatility of metal clay and the wide range of effects that can be achieved. From left to right: dichroic glass pendant by **Sara Dutton**, colourful resin pendants by **Kathleen Wickham**, blue dichroic glass pendant with lump clay by **Mary Cormican**, and finally a finger-printed heart with gold Keum-Boo by **Fleur Dutton**, age five, proving that metal clay really is for all ages and all levels of skill!

Suppliers and guilds

Suppliers

IN THE UK

Art Clay Supplies
2 Bakery Cottages,
Reading Road,
Burghfield Common,
RG7 3BS.
Tel: 0118 983 1071
(mail order only)
Suppliers of art clay, tools, kilns and courses

Learnsilverclay
Red Roofs, Jackies Lane
Newick
East Sussex BN8 4QX
Tel: 01825 722428
www.learnsilverclay.co.uk
Suppliers of metal clay, tools, and courses

MailleQueen
187 Hall Lane
Chingford
London E4 8HU
Tel: 020 8529 4213
www.maillequeen.co.uk
Suppliers of jump rings and chain maille kits

The PMC Studio
17 Chiltern Business Centre
63-65 Woodside Road
Amersham
Bucks HP6 6AA
Tel: 0870 8500151
Suppliers of precious metal clay, tools and kilns

PMC Workshops
Larkinglass Farm
Motcombe
Dorset SP7 9HY
Tel: 07989 300526
www.pmcworkshops.co.uk
Suppliers of metal clay, tools, and courses

Shiney Company
Unit 4.11– 4.12, Paintworks
Bath Road
Arnos Vale
Bristol BS4 3EH
Tel: 0117 300 9800
www.shineyrocks.co.uk
Suppliers of Swarovski crystals

Vitrum Signum
Gresham Works
Mornington Road
London E4 7DR
Tel: 020 8524 9546
www.vitrumsignum.co.uk
Enamel suppliers

Wires.co.uk
18 Raven Road
South Woodford
London E18 1HW
Tel: 020 8505 0002
www.wires.co.uk
Suppliers of fine silver and other wires

IN AUSTRALIA AND NEW ZEALAND

Ceramic and Craft Centre
Gary Ratcliffe
11 Green Street Revesby
NSW 2212
Australia
www.ceramicandcraft.com.au

Beadcharm
PO Box 10097
Adelaide St Brisbane
QLD 4000
Australia
www.beadcharm.com.au

Benjamins Crafts
868 Beaufort Street
Inglewood
WA 6052
Australia
Tel: 08 9370 2132
www.benjaminscrafts.com.au

Annie Rose Ltd
Judith Sleavin
187 Reyburn House Lane
Whangarei
New Zealand
Tel: 64 9 430 0817
www.annierose.com

Zigzag Polymer5 Clay Supplies
8 Cherry Place
Casebrook
Christchurch 8051
New Zealand
www.zigzag.co.nz

Guilds

FOR THE UK

Precious Metal Clay Guild UK
PO Box 219
Par
PL25 9AP
United Kingdom
Tel: 01726 816600
pmcguild.co.uk

Art Clay World Guild
131 Victoria Road
Diss
Norfolk
IP22 4JN
artclayworld.org.uk

FOR AUSTRALIA AND NEW ZEALAND

PMC Guild Australia and New Zealand
PO Box 7289, Bondi NSW 2026 Australia
17 Grange Street, Opawa Christchurch
New Zealand
www.pmcguild.com.au

Art Clay New Zealand Silver Guild
P.O.Box 89 123
Torbay
Auckland, 0742
09 473 3251

Glossary

These words are commonly used in the making of metal clay jewellery.

alloy a mixture of metals.

ball an attachment to your silver piece to allow you to fix a chain or ribbon to it.

bezel a metal band that can be soldered or fixed into metal clay to allow you to set non-fireable stones.

burnish to highly polish the silver.

casting grains small pellet-sized grains of precious metals, which can be used for decoration on metal clay.

cork clay a mouldable material that can be used to create hollow shapes and fired out in a kiln.

counter-enamel a layer of enamel applied to the back of the piece to stop distortion when fired.

cubic zirconia stones commonly known as cubic zirconias, these stone are man-made at very high temperatures and can be fired in a kiln and with a blowtorch. Not all cubic zirconias are colour stable and, to avoid disappointment, you should check with your supplier before firing.

dichroic glass glass that reflects one colour and transmits another. It is suitable for use with metal clay and must be fired in a kiln on a low-temperature, slow-fire programme.

engrave to carve a pattern into the dry metal clay with a cutting tool.

fine silver silver without any alloys added to it.

fire scale an oxidized layer in metal, which can be brushed off with a stainless steel brush.

glass brush a glass fibre brush used for cleaning silver before enamelling.

mandrel a wooden or metal shape used for building rings or bracelets on.

moulding compound a material that takes an excellent impression of objects to form a mould.

patina process where silver is coloured using a chemical agent, such as liver of sulphur and Platinol.

oxidization process that forms a discoloured layer of metal alloy over the surface of the metal through heat or when exposed to air over a period of time.

sintering where the product is just below melting point and when it acquires its strength.

Index

Acknowledgements

Thank you to my family for your help with all the boring bits so I could have fun writing this book. To my daughter, Fleur, who hasn't had much fun recently. To my dear friend Paula Louise Paton for her support in this project and her ability to make me laugh. To Amanda for your advice. To Thomas Sultana for his fantastic photographs (www.willowstone-photography.co.uk). To New Holland Publishers for asking me to write this book and for helping me along the way – I have learnt a lot.

To the lovely ladies who sent me their jewellery for the gallery: Jo Dix (Silver Forge, www.silverforge.co.uk); Mary Cormican (www.somata.co.uk); Paula Louise Paton (www.learnsilverclay.co.uk); Geraldine Mallinson (Skipton); Kathleen Wickham (Bath); and Fleur Dutton (aged 5)

To my aunt Jane MacLeod, who sat up through the night helping me, when I lost all my notes the day before my deadline. I really could not have done this without you.